Published by Carlton Books Ltd 2002

Carlton Books,
20 Mortimer Street,
London W1T 3JW.

Text Copyright © Howard Johnson 2002
Design Copyright © 2002 Carlton Books Ltd

ISBN 1 84222 749 1

A CIP catalogue for this book is available from the British Library.

Project Manager: Ian Gittins
Art Director: Clare Baggaley
Typeset by: Penny Dawes
Production: Sarah Corteel

CARLTON
BOOKS

# X-RATED
## the 200 RUDEST SONGS EVER!

Howard Johnson

PARENTAL
ADVISORY
EXPLICIT CONTENT

# X CONTENTS

# INTRODUCTION page 10

INTRODUCTION page 10

## X SONG TITLES

# X ALBUM SLEEVES

# X
# INTRODUCTION

If you're easily offended may I suggest you look away now. This is not a book for religious zealots, the faint-hearted, woolly-minded liberals or Tipper Gore. And it most definitely wouldn't have impressed Mary Whitehouse if the fanatical anti-filth merchant had been around to see it. *X-Rated: The 200 Rudest Songs Ever!* does exactly what it says on the tin. It brings you the handiest, most user-friendly dossier ever on the dirtiest, filthiest, lewdest, crudest, most sex-obsessed songs ever recorded. There is bad language, sexual content and nudity (often gratuitous) within these pages in what I believe is the definitive guide to musical muckiness. If the book were a movie it would most definitely be rated R18. And why has it been written? Well the glib answer would be because the songs, like Everest, were there. But really it's simply because sex goes with music like groupies go with everyone.

So what were the criteria used for inclusion in this file of filth? Well, it wasn't simply the tunes with the most dirty words that made the grade. That way some of the world's rudest ever recordings, which rely on innuendo (subtle or otherwise) rather than sheer graphic content wouldn't have made the cut. Then there's context to think about. If there's something surreptitiously saucy being released by what appears to be a clean-cut pop outfit, then that can sometimes have ruder repercussions than even the rawest rapper. And what about songs where it's the sounds rather than the actual words which elevate them to the very height of horniness? No self-respecting student of sonic sleaze could omit them, could they? Nor is there more than one entry per artist here. Surely that would be cheating. And it was decided that the content had to be about songs dealing with carnal doings, rather than numbers which simply use bad language. The book is about sex, not swearing, after all.

What I'm saying is that you'll just have to trust me on this. And if you don't like the choices, then why don't you e-mail me at rude.records@ntlworld.com and tell me which smutty songs should have made the cut — and why? Or maybe which songs that are included here couldn't make your sap rise in a month of Sundays. You never know, there might even be a follow-up. *X-Rated: The Readers' Choice*!

All the details and information provided are correct to the best of my knowledge and where possible I've given details of the album from which the tracks were taken. You will notice that some album entries do not correspond to the year of recording, as often tracks selected are only available on compilations released many years after the original recordings or indeed on singles alone. I hope this information is still helpful.

So go ahead and read the sordid details, the best lewd lines and the career consequences for 200 of the rudest recording artists ever to enter a studio. And if it's all a little bit blue, well don't say I didn't warn you!

Enjoy.

**Howard Johnson,
London 2002**


*People without whom...*

Louise, Elliott and Gabriel
Steve 'Steely Danglesey' Anglesey
Paul 'Gooner' Elliott
Robert 'King of Clubs' Swift
Ben Seaman
Alex McLellan

# AC/DC

## 'The Jack'
From *If You Want Blood, You've Got It* (Atlantic, 1978)

## STYLE

Tub-thumping, chest-beating, slow and low guitar blues designed to give its audience maximum nodability potential.

## THE SORDID DETAILS

Originally recorded by the Australian boogie band in 1975 for their Oz-only *T.N.T.* album, the true meaning of 'The Jack' was hidden behind the subtlest of metaphors. The girl in question "had the card to bring me down if she played it right". By the time of 1978's live classic, however, lead singer Bon Scott had re-written the words and thrown off any pretence that this was a song about anything other than getting a particularly nasty dose of the clap. If anyone was in any doubt, then Scott made it double clear by screaming "Gonorrhea" at the top of his battered and bruised voice before Angus Young launched into a typically heroic solo. Dumb, but fun.

## BEST LINE

"She was number nine ninety nine on the clicker list/And I fell in love with that dirty little bitch/She's got the jack."

## CAREER CONSEQUENCES

Quickly establishing itself as the centrepiece of the much-praised live album, AC/DC shook off any lingering doubts as to whether they were testosterone-heavy cobbers or not (AC/DC? A song called 'She's Got Balls'? A guitarist in short pants?) with this STD-centric anthem. And the kings of the musical equivalent of a smutty joke never looked back.

# AEROSMITH

### 'Big Ten Inch...'
From *Toys In The Attic* (Columbia, 1975)

## STYLE

Deliciously sleazy rag-time stomp which will surprise millions who only recognise Aerosmith as blow-dried MTV balladeers.

## THE SORDID DETAILS

Originally made notorious by '50s R'n'B performer Bull Moose Jackson, Aerosmith's 'Big Ten Inch...' is as sleazy a record as anything out there. Parping horns, rinky dink piano and a delivery of extraordinary lasciviousness from Steven Tyler highlight the qualities of this most un-hard rock-like hard rock band. Tyler has often referred to tracks that really move him as having "the jazz" and 'Big Ten Inch...' is surely the definitive aural explanation of the term. Chock full of juvenile plays on words and "glimmer in the eye" naughtiness, but delivered with such swagger and sass you'd have to be Mary Whitehouse or a member of The Smiths not to find yourself stirring down under when you hear this one.

## BEST LINE

"I, I, I cover her with kisses/And when we're in a lover's clinch/She gets all excited/When she begs for my big 10 inch.../Record of a band that plays those blues."

## CAREER CONSEQUENCES

Aerosmith's roller coaster career really took off after the success of 'Sweet Emotion' and 'Walk This Way' from *Toys In The Attic*, thereby giving Steven Tyler carte blanche to explore his seemingly endless fascination with the ladies. Clearly his own big ten inch has been called into action on a significant number of occasions, probably more so after giving up the potentially sexually debilitating mountain of drugs he freely admits to having ingested. When asked about groupies Tyler replied with a smile on his face and a simple "Love 'em!". Bless him.

# AKINYELE

## 'Pussy Makes The World Go Round'
From From *Aktapuss: The Soundtrack* (Volcano, 1999)

## STYLE
Relatively mellow, with lush synths and easy bass lines giving a laid-back feel that may surprise those who are expecting hardcore after hearing the title.

## THE SORDID DETAILS
Recorded as the soundtrack to the modern Blaxploitation movie *Aktapuss*, Akinyele Adams' third album features the usual old swearfest, though this time it's mixed with a more mellow musical backdrop than most hardcore rap records. Adams obviously has a more tender side to his personality than most are prepared to show, despite his regulation foul mouth. He actually seems to talk about love, though he's not averse to using gynaecological terminology to make his point. For girls who like guys who talk dirty, but who also want someone with soul.

## BEST LINE
"We could have a son or a daughter if you fuck me now/'Cos pussy makes the world go round."

## CAREER CONSEQUENCES
Akinyele is a long way short of superstar status, so maybe he's fallen between the two stools of smoochy and straight-up hardcore.

# ALI G AND SHAGGY

## 'Me Julie'
Single (Island, 2002)

## STYLE
Typical Shaggy-style Mr Loverman bits and bobs. Did he know this was actually a pastiche?

## THE SORDID DETAILS
Certainly sordid if you're talking about one cynical last scrape around the barrel of what was once a great comic invention. Sasha Baron Cohen's piss-take of the wigga mentality and the lack of understanding of youth culture in Britain's corridors of power was extremely funny. Until Cohen started to milk it. Shamelessly. This lame attempt to hype up the inevitable film has left Cohen with nowhere to turn. The premise of writing an ode to Ali's girlfriend with a few rude words for added street cred is laughable. Sadly, the record isn't funny. Knowing when to stop is the key to great comic creations and Cohen's timing is way, way off.

## BEST LINE
"Fitter than the Spice Girls including the Ginger/Give it a shave cause mi wanna be in ya/They was claiming that our love was wrong/The people just started and said it was too long/Yo it ain't a crime to have a 12-inch/Dong Da Dong Dong Dong."

## CAREER CONSEQUENCES
Utterly disastrous. From most loved to most sneered at in three-and-a-half minutes. That takes some doing.

 **GG ALLIN**

**'Be My Fucking Whore'**
From *Freaks, Faggots, Drunks And Junkies* (Awareness, 1988)

## STYLE
Amateurish, noise-infested and mercifully short.

## THE SORDID DETAILS
This man was clearly deranged. Allin was a legendary yet highly peripheral artist whose live shows were notorious for a variety of depraved acts, including crapping on stage, then eating it, carving his own flesh and forcing people's heads into his crotch. Not for the faint-hearted or those without strait-jackets, the man's music was just as confrontational – or stupid, depending on your view of this sort of behaviour. Did GG Allin get enough love as a child? Hard to say, but something had made him very, very angry indeed, as this track, randomly chosen from among a plethora of low-rent efforts, clearly proves.

## WORST LINES
"When I'm done I light a cigarette/And piss in your mouth/And then I'll kick you the fuck out/You little piece of worthless shit."

## CAREER CONSEQUENCES
"Musically he wasn't all that talented," explained Todd Phillips, the maker of Allin's 1993 documentary *Hated: GG Allin and the Murder Junkies* with admirable understatement. "He was pure evil too," he adds, helpfully. Perhaps he would have been as happy as anyone to have died of a heroin overdose in 1993, then.

# THE ANDREWS SISTERS

**'Rum & Coca Cola'**
From *The Best Of Andrews Sisters* (MCA, 1977)

## STYLE

Close knit harmonies from the three sisters who defined the jitterbug
and boogie-woogie style of the '40s.

## THE SORDID DETAILS

No, really, this is a rude record. After all, how many songs do you know
which celebrate a mother and daughter prostitution team?! It's hard to
imagine that the perma-grinning, squeaky clean Andrews Sisters were
really paying too much attention to the lyrics of their 1945 hit when
they were recording it. Otherwise they might not have felt too
comfortable explaining how things had become so much better in
Trinidad now that the Yankees had turned up and were paying for sex
left right and centre! The boogie woogie bugle boys of Company B were
getting their own horns blown for cash! Or at least that was the view of
lyricist and American comedian Morey Amsterdam. And the girls, bless
'em, just kept on singing!

## BEST LINES

"Out on Manzanella Beach/G.I. romance with native peach/All
night long, make tropic love/Next day, sit in hot sun and cool
off/Drinkin' rum and Coca-Cola/Go down Point Koomahnah/Both
mother and daughter/Workin' for the Yankee dollar."

## CAREER CONSEQUENCES

Never quite the draw they were in the war years, the sisters nonetheless
retained a huge degree of affection in American hearts

# ANTI NOWHERE LEAGUE

## 'So What?'
From *We Are...The League* (WXYZ, 1982)

## STYLE
Raucous and uselessly played three-chord punk thrash that was utterly unremarkable aside from singer Animal's mindless and mucky lyrics

## THE SORDID DETAILS
Designed originally to terrorise Tunbridge Wells in 1980, The Anti Nowhere League somehow ascended into the post punk mainstream, recorded a few shouty anthems and had their records seized by the Obscene Publications Squad. It all seems a bit much for a band that was hardly a threat to national security based on some very obviously "designed to shock" lyrics about buggering various beasts. Silly rather than sick, Animal and guitaring sidekick Magoo followed the Sex Pistols' credo of cash from chaos, though it's to be suspected that very little cash was ever seen before the intervention of a certain band from San Francisco.

## BEST LINES
"Well I fucked a sheep and I fucked a goat/I've had my cock right down its throat/So what, so what, you boring little cunt?"

## CAREER CONSEQUENCES
The usual tale of endless touring, various comings and goings and large dollops of bad behaviour (including the insertion of a carrot up one band member's rectum, apparently) before implosion. Animal candidly writes on his website biography alongside 1990 "WENT MAD". He was presumably saved by Metallica covering 'So What?' and royalties being delivered. Enough to get a taste again and reform the band.

# ANVIL

## 'Butter Bust Jerky'
From *Forged In Fire* (1983, Attic)

## X STYLE
Well, what do you think? Gut-pounding, no frills heavy metal with dirty riffs and even dirtier words.

## X THE SORDID DETAILS
Canadian quartet Anvil made something of a selling point of their rampant libidos. Led by guitarist and vocalist Lips (specialities, playing guitar with a vibrator, sporting bondage gear on stage), the band were to subtlety what Charles Manson is to comedy. All of their early records focused on sex – bi-sexual encounters, diseases and underage girls all feature on the lyrical agenda – but no one song captures the spirit of this band quite like 'Butter Bust Jerky'. Surely the only tune ever to espouse the joys of putting your penis between a large pair of breasts and using butter for lubrication, the sheer enthusiasm displayed by the band in their full-on delivery does them nothing but credit. Childish? Yes. Sexist? Obviously. Offensive? Only if you take such playground antics remotely seriously. And wear dungarees.

## X BEST LINES
"Dip your fingers in the butter/Spread it all across your chest/In between one another/You know what I like best/Push 'em close together/The tighter the better."

## X CAREER CONSEQUENCES
Clearly sex sells, though possibly not in huge quantities. Anvil passed the twenty-year mark in 2001 with the release of *Plenty Of Power*. Had they toned down? Sold out? Gone limp? Well, the cover features an enormous bulldozer, so what would your informed guess be?

# THE AU PAIRS

## 'Come Again'
From *Playing With A Different Sex* (Hurran, 1981)

## X STYLE
Deliberately difficult post punk from a band with a manifesto as much as a style.

## X THE SORDID DETAILS
Being fronted by a radical lesbian feminist may well have some impact on a band's songwriting stance, so it's no surprise that the Birmingham-based Au Pairs' first album was a confrontational beast. Lesley Woods clearly believed no subject was taboo and tackled gender roles and thorny political topics with uncompromising brutality. The album's cover image of two heavily armed women in what appears to be peasant dress charging across an open field in the midst of a conflict certainly made its point quickly and effectively. 'Come Again' dealt with the tricky subject of faking orgasms (particularly if you're a bloke) and the lack of interest shown by most men in their female partner's pleasure. Is this what turned Lesley?

## X BEST LINES *(male/female dialogue)*
"It's frustrating, aggravating/So annoying, pretend you're enjoying it."
"Am I doing it right?"
*(Er...I think the answer's no, mate!)*

## X CAREER CONSEQUENCES
Lesley Woods became a *Playboy* centrefold and married Hugh Hefner. Just joking. Since 1983's *Live In Berlin* nobody seems to have heard anything from the four band members. But we can safely assume that taking her clothes off for a men's magazine has not been Ms Woods' chosen career path.

# BALLOON

### 'Pussy Lovers'
From *Pussylovers* (Radikal, 2001)

## STYLE
Beat-tastic, bleep-mongous techno that clearly keeps the drug-addled BPM requirement up to speed.

## THE SORDID DETAILS
The German producer scored some commercial success with this six tracker featuring nothing but mixes of 'Pussy Lover'. The track had become a big hit for the big man (who weighs in at over 300 pounds) not only because of its provocative title, but also thanks to its excellent use of a sample from the film *From Dusk Till Dawn*, where a brothel owner describes his occupation in great detail. And given that Balloon is such a big guy, were you really going to come right out and tell him if you didn't like his record?

## BEST LINES
"Alright we got white pussy, black pussy, Spanish pussy, yellow pussy, hot pussy, cold pussy, wet pussy lovers/Attention pussy shoppers, take advantage of our penny pussy sale."

## CAREER CONSEQUENCES
The old hypnotic Eurobeats are bigger than big in, you guessed it, Europe, though Balloon has yet to, well, blow up anywhere else.

# BUJU BANTON

## 'Dickie'
From *Mr Mention* (Fader, 1993)

## STYLE
Fast and furious ragga style from a fast and furious ragga stylist.

## THE SORDID DETAILS
During the early-'90s Buju Banton was seen as a hate figure outside of his native Jamaica for his song 'Boom Boom Bye Bye', a vitriolic and violent attack on gays which incited violence toward them. Such a blunt approach to the issue outraged many who believed that Banton only made matters worse by refusing to apologise for his feelings. Of course, amid all the controversy over bashing gays, two things were overlooked. Firstly, his skills as a dancehall artist. And secondly, his sexually explicit lyrics. 'Dickie' has to be one of the most blatant odes to the power of the penis ever written and while the lyrics look utterly juvenile written down, there's no doubt that under Banton's control the song takes on an altogether more lascivious feel.

## BEST LINES
"Over the north and south and the east and the west/Gal them confess that dickie dickie is the best/Ann, who's your best friend?/She bawl out dick!"

## CAREER CONSEQUENCES
Since those heady early days Banton has calmed down, become a Rastaman and has even developed a social conscience, writing another childish song 'Willy (Don't Be Silly)', this time for the good cause of promoting the use of condoms. Maybe some of those who condemned him for his early outrages got through in the end.

23

# THE BEAUTIFUL SOUTH

## 'Don't Marry Her'
From *Blue Is The Colour* (Ark, 1996)

##  STYLE

Deceptively cheery pop that may well have astounded some of the band's more mainstream fans with its straight-to-the-point plea.

## THE SORDID DETAILS

Jacqueline Abbot has a voice that sounds so sweet you'd have sworn that nothing more naughty than a gobstopper had ever passed her lips. But the opening track on *Blue Is The Colour* would surely have had Beautiful South fans choking in their hot chocolate as Abbot delivered a soft-sounding song that was nevertheless full of all the bitterness and jealousy of love rivals – complete with the most Anglo-Saxon of pleas for sexual congress with the object of her affections. Following hot on the heels of the runaway success of *Carry On Up The Charts*, it was typically perverse of the band's main man Paul Heaton to offer something so unpalatable to mainstream tastes. But on such quirkiness The Beautiful South has existed for thirteen years.

## BEST LINES

"She'll grab your sweaty bollocks/Then slowly raise her knee/Don't marry her, fuck me."

## CAREER CONSEQUENCES

Well, the band recorded different lyrics for a single version ("Don't marry her, have me" – very tame) and doubtless some will see that as a cop out. Not that that will bother Paul Heaton any. Nor will the fact that the band's star appears to be in the descendant.

# BELL LABS SQUAD

## 'Yo Sister Sucked My Dick'
From *2001 – A Rap Odyssey* (Bell Labs, 2001)

## STYLE
Beats, rhymes, shouting, cussing, etc

## THE SORDID DETAILS
The Bell Labs Squad are dedicated to making "the most offensive, insane and illest rhymes and beats out there". Which is handy when you're writing toons about underage sisters giving head. If it's a joke it's a weak one. If it's serious it's sick, but with a band member rejoicing in the name of Ridiculous Rick With The Big Fucking Dick the likelihood of Bell Labs Squad being anything but offensive was always precisely nil.

## BEST LINES
"I don't like to eat bread/Your sister gave me head/I rode that redhead like a bobsled/After two servings, she was fed."

## CAREER CONSEQUENCES
Nobody had heard of them before, nobody has heard of them since.

# BERLIN

### 'Sex (I'm A...)'
From *Pleasure Victim* EP (Geffen, 1982)

## STYLE
Referred to at the time as 'Techno Slut', this is hi-energy, synthetic '80s pop cut with an atmosphere of seediness. Thankfully a million miles removed from the group's one monster hit, the ultra-slushy 'Take My Breath Away'.

## THE SORDID DETAILS
Berlin was set up to shock. A California band with a European name and sound, deliberately setting out to use sex as its mainstay theme, did not just happen by accident. Nor did the positioning of Terri Nunn as vocalist, having been a former teenage actress usually playing hookers, drug casualties and criminals. Onstage the inappropriately-named singer simulated fellatio and was credited on Pleasure Victim, with "Vocals, BJs". Well, it lubricates the vocal chords, presumably.

## BEST LINES
"Have you noticed that people are still having sex?/All the denouncement had absolutely no effect/Parents and councillors constantly scorn them/But people are still having sex and nothing seems to stop them."

## CAREER CONSEQUENCES
'Sex (I Am...)' was taken from the band's debut EP, which promptly went gold, again proving that as Spinal Tap so rightly claimed two years later, sex sells. Berlin's career as filth-mongers stalled dramatically after '86's 'You Take My Breath Away' piggybacked on the back of appearing on the enormous *Top Gun* movie soundtrack. Nunn left the band in 1987 to perv elsewhere, but was reunited with Berlin for 2000's back to bawdy *Berlin Live: Sacred & Profane*.

# CHUCK BERRY

## 'My Ding-A-Ling'
From *The London Sessions* (Chess, 1972)

## STYLE

Dumb and childish ditty, nursery-rhymish in feel, except for the lyrical allusions, of course.

## THE SORDID DETAILS

It must be the source of some irritation to Chuck Berry that he will forever be remembered by the mainstream solely as the perpetrator of this banal little number about his dick. Or as the bloke who was done for putting cameras in the ladies' loos in his restaurant. The man who redefined rock'n'roll guitar playing has contributed so much more to popular music, of course, but those are the risks you take when you record a novelty record. Berry's pedigree is unarguable. When Brian Wilson says Chuck wrote "all of the great songs and came up with all the rock'n'roll beats," then you know you're dealing with a rare talent. Yet 'My Ding-A-Ling' is as stupid as records get. The lyric isn't funny or interesting, the tune is banal. That's all there is to say.

## BEST LINES

"Now this here song it ain't so bad/Prettiest little song that you ever had/And those of you who will not sing/Must be playing with your own Ding-a-ling."

## CAREER CONSEQUENCES

Berry keeps on working and is no doubt more than comfortably off. But it's the aesthetic damage this tune has done that's the worry.

# IVOR BIGGUN AND THE RED NOSED BURGLERS

## 'The Winker's Song (Misprint)'
From *Fruity Bits Of Ivor Biggun* (Stiff Weapon Records, 2001)

## STYLE
Pastiche of the ukulele-driven remedial sound of George Formby. Only with really rude words, see...

## THE SORDID DETAILS
When this juvenile-beyond-belief song was released in the UK in 1978 it was naturally banned at once, playing into the hands (oh, this double entendre business is catching) of Mr Biggun by outraging all upstanding members (oh do stop it!) of society. The song, of course, is worthless, and while there's definitely a time and a place for a masturbation joke, allowing someone to base an entire recording career around it is surely taking things way too far. And just when you thought everyone had forgotten about this lame gag someone goes and writes a bloody book and puts it in!

## BEST LINES
"I was 25 years old before I was kissed/And then I found that I preferred a swift one off the wrist/It's cheap and convenient, you can't catch VD/It's available at any time and it's absolutely free."

## CAREER CONSEQUENCES
Help, there's a Biggun revival underway, with a new-ish album, *The Fruity Bits Of Ivor Biggun*.

# BITCH

## 'Live For The Whip'
From *Be My Slave/Damnation Alley* (Metal Blade, 1997)

## ✗ STYLE

Pacy heavy metal with the twist on the traditional themes being that lead vocalist Betsy was: a) a girl; and b) a dominatrix. The third twist, unfortunately, was that she couldn't sing.

## ✗ THE SORDID DETAILS

Betsy Bitch was the teenage fantasy of many a spotty metal fan when the harder rock sound suddenly began to gain in popularity in the early-'80s. Whether she was playing the whip-happy lassie for kicks or for real was never really known, but the sight of a busty girl dressed from head to toe in leather was more than enough to satisfy; Bitch's music much less so.

## ✗ BEST LINES

"The whip has involved you in life's little pleasures/Feel it all/Feel it all/Yeah, yeah/Live for the whip."

## ✗ CAREER CONSEQUENCES

Bitch's pedestrian riffing meant that they quite rightly floundered at the bottom of the metal genepool in their base of Los Angeles, and despite soldiering on for years they never made it any further. When placed next to bands such as W.A.S.P. and Mötley Crüe, their gimmick looked so cheap and amateurish it's hardly surprising.

# X BLINK 182

### 'Fuck A Dog'
From *Take Off Your Pants And Jacket* (MCA, 2001)

## X STYLE
Typically dumb Californian punk rock from a typically dumb
Californian punk rock band. Though clearly not too dumb to sell four
million copies of *Enema Of The State*.

## X THE SORDID DETAILS
The San Diego three piece have made something of a stock in trade of
their three piece pop punk anthems, often flecked with a healthy dose of
gratuitously crude lyrics. 'Fuck A Dog' is the finest example of said
style, plumbing new depths of grossness. The band clearly revel in
getting on the tits of anyone offended by anything and this song does
the job efficiently. Of course, let's not forget that being able to write a
song about bestiality and still be seen as "the cutesy punks it's OK to
like" is actually quite some achievement.

## X BEST LINES
"I tried to fuck your mom in the ass/I tried to fuck your dad in the
ass/Could only find the dog and his ass."

## X CAREER CONSEQUENCES
Nobody seems to have rumbled these three oiks yet and their career
continues to flourish. And why not? If Ozzy Osbourne can be invited to
the White House to meet George Bush these days, then anything but
anything is possible.

# THE BLOODHOUND GANG

## 'The Ballad Of Chasey Lane'
From *Hooray For Boobies* (Geffen, 2000)

## STYLE
Deliberately moronic rock that is expertly constructed to complement the numbskullian tendencies of the "titties and beer" lyrical obsessions.

## THE SORDID DETAILS
Glorying in idiocy is the entire raison d'etre of Pennsylvania's The Bloodhound Gang. They may well have an interest in commercial success (and they've had quite a chunk of it thanks to their 'The Bad Touch' hit), but they have absolutely no interest in attaining it by the usual means. If it ain't "spreading the gospel of fuck all" as he so brilliantly puts it, then band leader Jimmy Pop just isn't interested. Hence this specially-chosen love song of sorts, written from the perspective of an obsessed fan. Chasey Lane, in case you didn't know, is a top porno actress and she will no doubt be delighted with this touching tribute to her considerable naked talents.

## BEST LINES
"You've had a lotta dick/Had a lotta dick/I've had a lotta time/Had a lotta time/You've had a lotta dick, Chasey/But you ain't had mine."

## CAREER CONSEQUENCES
Well nobody knows just yet, but it's to be suspected that the proceeds from *Hooray For Boobies* should be enough to keep the band in whoopee cushions, itching powder and water-squirting bow ties for some considerable time yet.

# BLUE

### 'Too Close'
From *All Rise* (Innocent, 2001)

## STYLE
Slick-as-oil pop with necessary R'n'B undertow to give that much-needed whiff of credibility. Boy band, but clearly with attitude.

## THE SORDID DETAILS
For such a clean-cut act this is a very rude song indeed. It makes you wonder if parents really know what's going on in their teenage daughters' bedrooms. Blue positively glow with health and efficiency and this recording sparkles with the perma-white sheen of pop toothpaste. But beneath those impeccable harmonies there are some grubby thoughts going on, involving, frankly, erections. And any song that can use the word "sexing" as a verb ("It's almost like we're sexing") can't be too bad, can it?

## BEST LINES
"I try but I can't hide it/You're dancing real close/Plus it's real, real slow/You're making it hard for me."

## CAREER CONSEQUENCES
Like kids in the playground getting away with something, it appears that Blue have yet to be taken to task over their "parental advisory" lyrics and number one singles have been effortlessly delivered. How they've managed this (their album's titled *All Rise*, for heaven's sake!) without getting into terrible trouble from our moral guardians is beyond a sane man's understanding.

# THE BOMB PARTY

## 'Fist Fucking Baby'
From *Monsters of Goth* (Cleopatra compilation, 1997)

## STYLE

Garage rock that's unsophisticated even by garage rock standards.
Really lo-fi.

## THE SORDID DETAILS

Taking their name from a Graeme Greene novel displayed some literary
tendencies, but The Bomb Party's musical style was far less cerebral and
much more direct. Lumped in with the UK goth movement when they
sounded more like a biker band, The Bomb Party had an unerring
ability to shock and knew how to play up to it. The first album,
released in 1986, was titled *Drugs*. But the band had a sense of humour,
albeit warped – the second album was called *Liberace Rising*. Some
people may have been shocked by the fact that a group, which included
a girl, Sarah Corina, could record such a sexually graphic song as 'Fist
Fucking Baby', but it's unlikely that the lady herself would have
thanked you for such hand-wringing concern on her behalf.

## BEST LINES

"Uh gurd lerkin fist ferkin babeeya/Uh gurd lerkin fist ferkin
babeeya/ Uh gurd lerkin fist ferkin babeeya/Uh gurd lerkin fist
ferkin babeeya."

## CAREER CONSEQUENCES

Besides death and taxes the only certain thing in life is that The
Bomb Party would not become a major commercial success. They split
in 1990.

# MICHAEL 'BOOGALOO' BOYER

**'Slob On My Knob'**
From *Ghetto, House, Booty Tracks Volume 1* (Smoked Out, 2000)

## STYLE

Repetitive hard dance groove. Repetitive hard dance groove. Repetitive hard dance groove. (Get the idea?)

## THE SORDID DETAILS

Our friend "Boogaloo" is apparently one of the hottest DJs in Memphis, ("six till midnight on Hot 107, cruisers") and in his spare time what he likes to do more than anything else is put out albums rammed to the gills with dirty titles and dirty lyrics. *Ghetto...* is a veritable treasure chest of opportunity for the filthy-minded. 'Put This Dick In Your Mouth', 'Bitches And Hos' and the unforgettable 'Slob On My Knob' are all part of the Boyer repertoire. And all this from a man who's on air before the nine o'clock watershed!

## BEST LINES

"Slob on my, slob on my, slob on my, slob on my, slob on my knob."

## CAREER CONSEQUENCES

Like I said, he's one of the hottest DJs in Memphis. And he sometimes DJs at the Hard Rock Café there. It don't get bigger than that!

# JOHNNY BRISTOL

## 'Hang On In There Baby'
From *Best Of Johnny Bristol* (Polydor, 1978)

## STYLE
Deceptively smooth and sincere pop soul groove that means if you take your eye off the ball for a minute you might not notice what dark doings are actually going on here.

## THE SORDID DETAILS
Johnny Bristol made his name as a writer/producer at the Motown hit factory in Detroit in the '60s and early-'70s, helping pen such classics as 'Ain't No Mountain High Enough' and 'Help Me Make it Through The Night'. But it wasn't until 1974 and a solo deal with MGM that Bristol really became a star in his own right. 'Hang On In There Baby' was his first single and immediately became a massive hit, despite the fact that the lyrics were, not to put too fine a point on it, about deflowering a virgin. Don't believe it? "Hang on in sweet virgin of the world...Oh, right there, right there. Baby, don't you move it anywhere.". Now can you see why Love God Gary Barlow had to have a stab at it?!

## BEST LINES
"Don't fight it baby, open up the door/'Cos that's the key to freedom/That we've both been working for/Let it go baby, let it go honey/Oh, right there, right there/Baby, don't you move it anywhere."

## CAREER CONSEQUENCES
Never really bettered this classic moment. Bristol has kept working, recording and writing, but this dastardly hit will always be his tour de force.

# JAMES BROWN

## 'Get Up (I Feel Like Being A) Sex Machine'
From *Sex Machine* (King, 1970)

## STYLE
Superfly funk delivered with that trademark nasty, nasty vocal from the self-proclaimed "Godfather Of Soul".

## THE SORDID DETAILS
No-one has earned the right to call themselves a legend quite as much as James Brown. Revolutionary, criminal, civil rights activist, dirtbag, Brown is all of these things and more, an acolyte of music who burns with desire to bring it to the people – groovier, more soulful and funkier than anyone else ever. The shadow he casts over the evolution of black music is long and his live performances are the benchmark by which all others must be judged. And for a man who's now in his sixties Brown still remains cooler than cool, rawer than raw and ruder than most. Yes, there are dirtier lyrics around by far. Yes, there are more sexually alluring performers out there. But for sheer, downright in-the-groove, raw sexual energy, this eleven-minute live version of 'Get Up...' is a tough cookie to beat. Be careful. Playing this record when juiced up can lead to irresponsible behaviour.

## BEST LINES
"Get up, get on up/Get up, get on up/Stay on the scene/Like a sex machine." *(Repeat at least two hundred times.)*

## CAREER CONSEQUENCES
Brown's career took a dive in the mid-'70s as disco took a hold, but the emergence of rap saw Soul Brother Number One rehabilitated through collaborations and endless sampling of his funky grooves. A prison sentence following allegations of assault and battery by his wife and an interstate police car chase only served to enhance the Brown legend.

# JIMMY BUFFET

## 'Why Don't We Get Drunk'
From *A White Sport Coat And A Pink Crustacean*
(MCA, 1973)

##  STYLE
Lonesome cowboy country with plenty of harp-parping for added pathos.

##  THE SORDID DETAILS
Don't be fooled by the "I'm a bit of a loser and could sure use a break" feel of this little number. Jimmy Buffet is one of the highest-earning entertainers out there thanks to an empire comprising recordings, clothing and nightclubs… which just goes to show that being a West Coast beach bum can pay dividends. Buffet's career has been an up and down affair, but when he's hit he's hit big. This tune is part of his pre-fame catalogue (his first singles chart entry was actually a year later, in 1974) and so we can at least believe the straightforward sentiment could be genuine.

##  BEST LINES
**"I really do appreciate the fact you're sittin' here/Your voice sounds so wonderful/But yer face don't look too clear/So barmaid bring a pitcher, another round o'brew/Honey, why don't we get drunk and screw?"**

##  CAREER CONSEQUENCES
This wasn't the song that did it for Buffet. That honour went to 1977's 'Margaritaville' above all, but it'd be nice to pretend he's still a dirty penniless bum looking to get his leg over, wouldn't it?

# BULL MOOSE JACKSON

'Nosey Joe'
From *Final Recordings* (Bogus Recordings, 1992)

## STYLE
Jump blues that swings so much it absolutely, positively hurts.

## THE SORDID DETAILS
Benjamin Jackson was nicknamed Bull Moose because some of his contemporaries on the '40s blues scene thought that he, well, looked like one. The man must have been a placid fellow, because not only did he not tear their heads off, he even adopted his new nickname to show there were no hard feelings. Could it be that Bull Moose's inner calm all came from the fact that one of his main hits, 'Big Ten Inch...', was sung out of joyful experience? Who knows? Whatever, Bull Moose was partial to the old innuendo as 'Nosey Joe' (incredibly written by Lieber & Stoller!) ably demonstrates. Subtle it is not, but those who think that society has become that much more crude over the last couple of decades need only glance at the lyrics below to realise that there's always been someone ready to put their pervy credentials up for inspection. Well done, son.

## BEST LINES
"There's a man in town all the women know/He goes by the name of Nosey Joe/He don't care if they're married/He takes his pick/Long as they're women, he's ready to stick/His big nose in their business."

## CAREER CONSEQUENCES
Bull Moose managed well enough maintaining both a pop career as a crooner and a jump blues life complete with risqué lyrics. Although he faded from the scene there was a slight revival with Moosemania propagated by a Pittsburgh band called The Flashcats, but sadly the man died of lung cancer in 1989 aged 70.

# BUZZCOCKS

## 'Orgasm Addict'
From *Singles Going Steady* (United Artists, 1979)

## STYLE
Punk with a pure pop twist. Slashing guitars counterpoint the campy vocals of Pete Shelley to produce a classic.

## THE SORDID DETAILS
Inspired by The Sex Pistols, Manchester's Buzzcocks nevertheless took the punk theme and twisted it through ninety degrees to offer something new. Pete Shelley's tales of adolescent angst, brought on by an onrush of hormones, were almost sweet in their naïvety. Many staid institutions, however, disagreed, and radio refused to play the band's first single 'Orgasm Addict' in October of 1977. Shelley's colourful description of the teenage jerk fiend who graduates to full-on lothario lacked much of punk's vitriol, but still carried the movement's ethic of being able to shock. To Shelley's credit the theme of masturbation and its attendant problems didn't appear to be forced. It probably made a lot of spotty boys feel better about their solo bedroom manoeuvres too.

## BEST LINES
"Sneakin' in the back door with dirty magazines/And your mother wants to know what those stains are on your jeans/You're an orgasm addict."

## CAREER CONSEQUENCES
Built to be throwaway, The Buzzcocks imploded like all good punk bands should have done and by 1981 it was all over for the original line-up. Various solo efforts met with varying degrees of success and the band was reunited in the '90s – though, as you can imagine, the thrill of a middle-aged band singing about masturbation was somewhat less appealing.

# CANDY SNATCHERS

## 'Ass Casserole'
From *This Is Rock'n'Roll* (split album with Cheap Dates)
(Man's Ruin, 2001)

##  STYLE
Frenetic and wild fuzzed-up rock'n'roll, which makes up in enthusiasm what it lacks in finesse.

##  THE SORDID DETAILS
Virginia's Candy Snatchers once had a review written about them which quite brilliantly said: "In a word, they're fucking dangerous"! If this is the level of their journalistic supporters, then what must their fans be like? 'Ass Casserole' is an enthusiastic tribute to the booty and is possibly the only song ever written about sex to feature the word "culinary", though to be fair this fact hasn't been rigorously checked. No matter, if butt and buzzsaw guitars is your thing, then you will find this lot most righteous indeed.

##  BEST LINES
"She's got the ass cass-er-ole." *(This is surely the greatest phonetic pronunciation of the word 'casserole' ever attempted. The man is clearly a professional.)*

##  CAREER CONSEQUENCES
Jamie Oliver hasn't offered an 'Ass Casserole' recipe in one of his books just yet.

# CANNIBAL CORPSE

## 'Fucked With A Knife'
From *The Bleeding* (Metal Blade, 1994)

## STYLE
Deliberately gross, provocative, sexually violent lyrics. Don't do them the favour of being outraged.

## THE SORDID DETAILS
This Buffalo, New York death metal band saw a gap in the market — being the grossest of the gross — and went for it. Bully for them, it doesn't make them any less cheap and puerile for it. There's no merit in this dunderheaded attempt to shock. The band's songs simply weren't good enough to merit any mainstream attention, which meant that Cannibal Corpse were preaching to the converted, making records for spotty virgins who couldn't get a shag and thus were reduced to fantasising about violent sexual scenarios. Pathetic music for pathetic people.

## WORST LINES
"She liked the way it felt inside her/Fucking her, harder, harder."

## CAREER CONSEQUENCES
Big fish in a very small pond, Cannibal Corpse have singularly failed to trouble the mainstream, which is doubtless the way they (and certainly we) like it.

# RODNEY CARRINGTON

**'Letter To My Penis'**
From *Hangin' With Rodney* (Mercury Nashville, 1998)

## ◪ STYLE

Country comedy from a man who says he's not out to shock, just to talk about the things we all discuss in private. A public service guy, really.

## ◪ THE SORDID DETAILS

Rodney Carrington was raised in the Texas town of Longview and claims to produce the kind of material that has never been heard on a country music label before. What he means is he'll say the words "penis" and "bastard" and hang the consequences. His debut album *Hangin' With Rodney* needed the first ever "Explicit Lyrics" sticker for a country album – an accolade of which he's rightly proud. He then says: "I don't consider my act dirty," which means he's both rude and confused.

## ◪ BEST LINES

*(This is the penis talking, by the way):* "Dear Rodney, I don't think I like you anymore/'Cos when you get to drinkin' you put me places I've never been before/Dear Rodney, I don't like you anymore."

## ◪ CAREER CONSEQUENCES

It's the big time for the coarse countryman. Albums on top of the comedy charts, sold-out gigs, "full production show" for God's sake! That's penis power for you.

# JASPER CARROT

## 'Magic Roundabout'
Single (DJM, 1975)

## ▨ STYLE

Part musical, mainly spoken comedy effort based around the notion that the characters in a kids' TV show might be at it like rabbits. Laughing yet?

## ▨ THE SORDID DETAILS

Hard to believe that nice, middle-of-the-road BBC stalwart Jasper Carrot could ever have been considered at the cutting edge of anything. But at one time in the early-'70s Carrot was considered alternative. This could have had more to do with his shoulder length hair than his comic content, but that may be harsh, as this B-side to hit single 'Funky Moped' (produced by ELO man Jeff Lynne, incredibly!) sort of proves. Check out the swear words. Thrill to the naughtiness. Be glad you weren't old enough to "enjoy" such high class entertainment.

## ▨ BEST LINES

"I wonder if Florence is a virgin?/'Drops 'em for certain,' said Dylan/Booinngg!"

## ▨ CAREER CONSEQUENCES

The bright lights of television beckoned shortly after 'Funky Moped' and Carrot was soon to leave this puerile music-making way behind.

# BO CARTER

## 'Banana In Your Fruit Basket'
From *Banana In Your Fruit Basket* (Yazoo, 1978)

##  STYLE

Average guitar-picking blues that makes you sit up and take notice because it's so transparently titillating

## THE SORDID DETAILS

Of all the blues artists performing in the '20s and '30s who were hooked on none-too-subtle sexual innuendo, Bo Carter could justifiably claim the title of The Daddy! Born Bo Chatmon on March 21, 1893 into a musical family in Mississippi (where just the thirteen children showed musical talent!), Carter's list of blue songs would have had Mary Whitehouse turning the same shade herself and probably still wouldn't get radio airplay today due to sheer naughtiness. 'Mashing That Thing', 'Don't Mash My Digger So Deep', 'Pin In Your Cushion', 'My Pencil Won't Write Anymore'… the list goes on and it didn't take a sleuth to work out what Bo was on about. Still, 'Banana In Your Fruit Basket' remains his most famous X-rated effort for what are surely obvious reasons. Carter's style may not have been the most original, but his choice of subject matter showed he was a shrewd judge of what the people want – then, now and forever!

## BEST LINES

"Now I've got the white clothes, my baby got the tub/Gonna put them together, gonna rub rub rub/Let me put my banana in your fruit basket and I'll be satisfied."

## CAREER CONSEQUENCES

Enjoyed a long career as a solo artist, as well as in The Memphis Sheiks with his brothers Lonnie and Sam. Died in 1964 aged 67.

# DEANA CARTER

## 'Did I Shave My Legs For This?'
From *Did I Shave My Legs For This?* (Capitol Nashville, 1995)

## STYLE
Good ol' girl delivery with good ol' boy backing of rinky-tink piano and lap pedal steel for this stylish country "My man done me wrong" kinda song.

## THE SORDID DETAILS
Not really a rude lyric, but definitely a rude implication – and a funny one at that, thereby getting it the green light. Deana Carter's debut caused a real stir when it was released in 1995 on the back of the title track, a humorous look at the oafishness of men with a pay-off line that makes guys laugh and women nod knowingly (and possibly crossly). The daughter of Nashville studio guitarist Fred Carter Jr, Deana only learnt to play guitar aged 23, but soon secured a deal on the back of quirky, spirited songs like this. And having looked at her picture any bloke who'd rather have a beer than settle down to a night of headboard-banging action with this girl needs his head examining.

## BEST LINES
"I bought these new heels, did my nails/Had my hair done just right/I thought this new dress was a sure bet for romance tonight/Well it's perfectly clear, between the TV and beer/I won't get so much as a kiss/As I head for the door I turn around to be sure/Did I shave my legs for this?"

## CAREER CONSEQUENCES
A gold album for your debut isn't too shabby, now, is it?

# CHEAP TRICK

## 'Daddy Should Have Stayed In High School'
From *Cheap Trick* (Epic, 1977)

## STYLE
Pop rock with a twist – in this case a sinister undertone.

## THE SORDID DETAILS
These longstanding pop-rock activists have often hidden a more cynical and sordid side underneath their infectious melodies, and nowhere more so than on the band's first album, recorded with legendary figure Jack Douglas in 1976. Far from trying to satisfy a commercial agenda it seems as if the Illinois four piece were determined to sabotage their naturally commercial sound by dealing with some close-to-the-knuckle subject matter. 'Daddy...' is a disturbing and dirty song about a 30-year-old's infatuation with a schoolgirl which leads to something altogether more nasty. The band don't spare the listener the sordid details, but at no point does it appear as if they are glorying in the schoolyard pervert's depraved behaviour.

## BEST LINES
"Sorry that I had to gag you/You look better completely undressed/Sorry but I had to have you/I'm 30 but I feel like 16 might even be your daddy/I'm thinking more than a kiss/Whip me, spank me, grab me."

## CAREER CONSEQUENCES
Cheap Trick's uncanny ability to fuse their natural poppiness with something a little more sleazy has stood them in good stead, delivered one all-time classic in *Live At Budokan*, and kept the band working right through to the present day.

 **CHEF**

## 'Chocolate Salty Balls (PS I Love You)'
From *Chef Aid: The South Park Album* (Columbia, 1998)

## STYLE
Smooth as, well, chocolate soul delivered with effortless grace and heavily disguised irony by Isaac Hayes. Peeping from underneath a chef's hat, presumably.

## THE SORDID DETAILS
South Park was the lo-fi American animation that caught everyone's eye after the cussin'n'metal success of *Beavis and Butt-head*. Even stupider and cruder – in design and execution – South Park's take on the horrors that exist within a child's mind cleverly stitched in cameos from famous folk, including soul legend Isaac Hayes playing the role of the love-hungry school chef. The track itself was based around the most low rent of innuendoes, but such was the infatuation with juvenile humour at the time it proved a massive hit, with grown men crying with mirth at the irony of it all.

## BEST LINES
"Oooo suck on my chocolate salted balls/Stick 'em in your mouth and suck em!/Suck on my chocolate salted balls/They're packed full of vitamins and good for you/So suck on my balls."

## CAREER CONSEQUENCES
Only good news for the super-smooth soul brother, who was consequently hailed not only as one of the greatest singers of all time, but as a man who could clearly laugh at himself. Harmless, childish fun, but hardly a song to cherish.

# CHRISTIAN DEATH

**'Fucking In Slow Motion'**
From *Born Again Anti Christian* (Cleopatra, 2001)

## STYLE
Ponderous and miserable goth rock for the ponderous and miserable among you.

## THE SORDID DETAILS
Christian Death have always been hailed as one of the spiritual leaders of the goth scene despite never attained anything like the levels of commercial success enjoyed by, say, Bauhaus. This could have something to do with their excessively dull take on gloom, their exceedingly wearing banging on about how bad organised religion is (yes, we get the message) and quite possibly titles like this, which will certainly see off the part-timers in the scene. There are clearly no frisbees allowed in the Christian Death camp and even going at it like jackrabbits seems to be reduced to the level of a carnal chore. It almost makes you want to join the church.

## BEST LINES
"Rejecting shriek of pain/Fucking you in slow motion/Infecting" ...and other jolly notions.

## CAREER CONSEQUENCES
Plodding on, despite numerous line-up changes and the departure of vocalist Rozz Williams for a solo career in 1995. The career never got off the ground. He committed suicide in 1998.

# CIRCLE JERKS

## 'Group Sex'
From *Group Sex* (Epitaph, 1980)

## STYLE
Fast and deliberately idiotic bastardization of the original punk format that relies on frenetic riffing, shouty vocals and songs lasting a minute and a bit tops.

## THE SORDID DETAILS
Formed by Black Flag vocalist Keith Morris with the intention of shocking through stupidity (as if you couldn't get that from the group's name!), the band's debut album, *Group Sex*, pretty much achieved its goal. Featuring fourteen songs spewed out in just sixteen minutes, the majority of the album is somewhat comic book in approach, especially the title track, where a radio-style ad for swinging California parties is interspersed with the words "group sex" shouted and then shouted again. As irony goes you might well call it a bit heavy-handed, but there's no denying that it has a certain moronic charm. It's not revealed whether any of the band members have ever actually had group sex, but judging by the heavy testosterone at work here, it's almost certain they would have wanted to.

## BEST LINES
"Private swing party Friday and Saturday night/Wouldn't it be nice to have a party with couples that are friendly and mellow?/A low-key atmosphere where you can explore your most sensual fantasies with other aware sensitive couples."

## CAREER CONSEQUENCES
Nothing much developed outside of the group's core surfer and stoner fan base, but they did record a version of the Soft Boys' 'I Wanna Destroy You' on the 1995 album *Oddities, Abnormalities and Curiosities* with vocals contributed by former pop flossie Debbie Gibson, no less.

# DAVID ALLAN COE

## 'Cum Stains On My Pillow'
From XXX *Underground* (Bootleg, 1980)

## X STYLE
Bawdy country from a man who can only be described as a Bad Old, Good Old Boy.

## X THE SORDID DETAILS
Now in his sixties, David Allan Coe is a genuine rebel and outlaw. Sent to reform school at the age of nine, he was in and out of a variety of correctional facilities up to the age of 30, when he decided he'd prefer to be a musician and pitched up in Nashville where he immediately started living out of the back of a hearse. Eventually, Coe's gritty songs started to gain acceptance and Johnny Paycheck's cover of 'Take This Job And Shove It' made it to Number One in 1977. However, Coe also recorded a number of X-rated tunes that have only appeared on bootleg – including this salty little chap.

## X BEST LINES
"Now there's cum stains on the pillow where she once laid her head."

## X CAREER CONSEQUENCES
Coe is still hanging in there, looking mad as a snake, still making records and still respected by the country community as a bona fide outlaw. And he's probably still rude.

# LEONARD COHEN

## 'Don't Go Home With Your Hard On'
From *Death Of A Ladies' Man* (Warner Bros, 1977)

## STYLE
Cohen goes jaunty! Not at all the usual world-weary laconic fare from Canada's most memorable mumbler.

## THE SORDID DETAILS
Many people feel that *Death Of A Ladies' Man* was one of Cohen's least successful efforts, mainly due to the bizarre choice of Phil Spector as producer. The idea of mixing the Canadian singer's bleak monotone and sparse delivery with the producer's famed "Wall Of Sound" produced an ugly clash of styles. In many ways the most enduring moment on the album was this particular song title and its curious tale of a man born in a beauty salon. It's impossible to make sense of the lyrics, but the often repeated refrain of "You can't melt it down in the rain" will stick with you like glue.

## BEST LINES
"Ah, but don't go home with your hard-on/It will only drive you insane/You can't shake it (or break it) with your Motown/You can't melt it down in the rain."

## CAREER CONSEQUENCES
Well, it could be said with some certainty that the order of monks that Cohen has been spending much of his time with over the last few years will probably not have been playing this particular number at evensong. Though if Robbie Williams can be ordained a priest it's possible that anything can happen.

# COLOR ME BADD

**'I Wanna Sex You Up'**
From *CMB* (Giant, 1991)

## X STYLE
Slick vocal harmony humper from multi-racial R'n'B-ers

## X THE SORDID DETAILS
This Oklahoma four-piece met as high school students and relocated to New York before scoring a major deal and hitting the jackpot almost straight out of the box. 'I Wanna Sex You Up' was featured on the soundtrack to the hip *New Jack City* movie and immediately catapulted Color Me Badd to superstardom. The tune was your usual "I'm going to do it to you tonight, because I'm dead good at it, you know..." fare, possibly given an edge over the competition because of its blatant lyrical content and the fact that the band looked sufficiently non-threatening to appeal to the middle ground.

## X BEST LINES
"Girl you just make me feel so good/I just wanna... I just wanna/Just lay back, and enjoy the ride/All I wanna do is (I Wanna Sex You Up)/I Want to sex you up all night."

## X CAREER CONSEQUENCES
A three million-selling debut and six consecutive Top 20 hits meant that Color Me Badd were pop's 1992 darlings. But as is the way with pop sensations the success couldn't last and the group disbanded before the decade was out.

# WAYNE COUNTY

## 'Fuck Off'
From *The Electric Chairs* (Safari French Version, 1978)

## STYLE
Trashy, New York Dolls-influenced punk rock from a Georgian drag artist who soon went the whole transsexual route and became Jayne County in 1980.

## THE SORDID DETAILS
With a wig as big as Dolly Parton's, an in-your-face attitude and the tiniest modicum of ability, Wayne County was forced out of his more conservative American homeland to find recognition of sorts in London at the height of the punk boom. Always a curiosity rather than a front line talent, County shocked and stunned more than he rocked and rolled, and if it hadn't been for the gender-bending nature of his act and the full-on foul-mouthery of his best-known endeavour, it's doubtful he would have made much of an impression.

## BEST LINES
"If you don't want to fuck me/Then baby fuck off."

## CAREER CONSEQUENCES
Well, she was never going to be mainstream, was she? Nonetheless, Jayne County is still just about active in the music business and has a small, but dedicated band of fans who post truly hot information on websites such as: 'Jayne has a new evening look of black hair & black Cleopatra eye make-up.' And there ain't many artists who can inspire that kind of loyalty!

# IDA COX

## 'One Hour Mama'
From *Can't Quit That Man* (Affinity, 1939)

## STYLE

Bold as brass raunchiness from a woman you wouldn't want to mess with.

## THE SORDID DETAILS

Georgia girl Ida was singing in theatres by the time she was 14, travelling the south and entertaining as both a singer and comedienne. After working with Jelly Roll Morton in the early '20s Cox signed to Paramount and recorded with the label for six years. 'One Hour Mama' is as close to a girl power anthem as you can get from a time when the only Cox that was allowed to be mentioned was in the artist's surname. Clearly, Ida was a lady who knew how she wanted to be, er, serviced, and was not about to settle for any measures that were, well, "half-cock".

## BEST LINES

"I'm a one hour mama so no one minute papa/Ain't the kind of man for me/I can't stand no greenhorn lover like a rookie gone to war/With a load of big artillery but don't know what it's for."

## CAREER CONSEQUENCES

Alongside many of the other great blues singers of the era Cox suffered during the '30s due to the sudden dip in popularity of blues music, but she kept working right up until a stoke forced her into retirement in 1944. She came back to record one final session as late as 1961, but sadly died of cancer in 1967.

# THE CRAMPS

## 'Can Your Pussy Do The Dog?'
From *Date With Elvis* (New Rose, 1986)

## STYLE

Wang, twang, sweet poontang! Revved up rockabilly recommended for freaks everywhere.

## THE SORDID DETAILS

Lux Interior and Ivy Rorschach have been peddling their own unique brand of '50s rockabilly mixed with sexual fetishism and B-movie gore obsession for over twenty-five years now. If they've got bored of it all they've yet to show it and have been responsible for some of the most stupid and fun tunes ever to have come out of the alternative field. With Interior's self-consciously stylised vocals and Rorschach's twanging guitar riffs there's not much chance of anyone taking their lewd suggestions remotely seriously. But as far as re-energising the glamorous world of '50s sex sirens and infusing something altogether more, well, perverted into the mix, The Cramps have done a damn fine job.

## BEST LINES

"Yeah, let's see you wag that tail, now, woah, ya, Ya, ya /You're looking good now baby, just like I knew you would/Yeah, come on now, roll over baby, that's right/Let's try it this way for a while/Mmm, mmm, yeah, now fetch this!"

## CAREER CONSEQUENCES

Not so much a career as a vocation, Interior and Rorschach will probably still be making this bizarre swamp music even after nuclear holocaust.

# CRAZY TOWN

### 'Lollipop Porn'
From *The Gift of Game* (Sony, 1999)

## STYLE
Catchy rock rap blend from LA sons of music industry types.

## THE SORDID DETAILS
Crazy Town main men Seth "Shifty Shellshock" Binzer and Bret "Epic" Mazur are the sons of the director of the live Rolling Stones movie *Ladies And Gentlemen: The Rolling Stones* and Billy Joel's manager respectively. Their music, however, is a not a cross of bluesy leering and bug-eyed piano plonking, but rather a muscular white tribute to metal riffs and Compton gangsta posturing. So far so horrible, except that it isn't. Crazy Town defy the odds by turning in a deft modern rock sound – if you can use the word deft with lyrical matter as grime-ridden as this, that is. Just your everyday tale of a (presumably) underage porno star with a death wish, then. Out of such unpromising material something worthwhile has emerged.

## BEST LINES
"I got a lollipop porn bitch/Dead on arrival/A hardcore sex bitch turned suicidal/I got a lollipop porn bitch/Dead on arrival/A hardcore sex bitch turned suicidal."

## CAREER CONSEQUENCES
Crazy Town's reputation hasn't been founded on the back of this smutty little number, but rather the cuddly and fluffy 'Butterfly', a sentimental song about a beautiful laydee. But judging by Shifty's enormous tattoo collection you kind of knew he had this in him, didn't you?

# JIM DANDY AND BLACK OAK ARKANSAS

## 'I Want A Woman With Big Titties'
From *The Black Attack Is Back* (Heavy Metal, 1986)

## STYLE

One-eye-in-the-middle-of-the-forehead southern rock that clearly doesn't subscribe to the "We leave it up to the listener to interpret the lyrics" school of thought.

## THE SORDID DETAILS

James "Big Jim Dandy" Mangrum was the prototype for such '80s stadium rock frontmen as David Lee Roth and Vince Neil. Naming his band after the town of his birth, Mangrum made up for a lack of musical finesse in the ranks with testosterone-fuelled energy, a desire to sing about sex all the time, a washboard (which he used for spirited solos!) and the tightest white pants this side of the Royal Ballet. Against all odds Black Oak enjoyed some success in the '70s and even managed a Top 30 US hit with a cover of LaVern Baker's 'Jim Dandy To The Rescue'. 'I Want A Woman With Big Titties' dates from the mid-'80s, by which time Black Oak's appeal had become very much more selective. Mangrum's enthusiasm for the band's core theme of sex, however, is blatantly undiminished.

## BEST LINES

"I want a woman with big titties." (*What could possibly better that?*)

## CAREER CONSEQUENCES

Not exactly a radio favourite, 'I Want A Woman With Big Titties' no doubt played well in frat houses across America, but failed to re-ignite the Black Oak commercial fires. Mangrum, now aged 54, is still touring with his latest Black Oak line-up. Complete with washboard!

# DEAD KENNEDYS

## 'Too Drunk To Fuck'
From *Give Me Convenience Or Give Me Death*
(Alternative Tentacles, 1987)

## STYLE
Lambasting punk rock designed to offend those people who will always get offended by other people saying "fuck" in public places.

## THE SORDID DETAILS
Mixing politics and punk in '80s America was a dangerous business and The Dead Kennedys mixed it more than most. Their name alone would have been enough to cause palpitations among good Christian folk, but leader Jello Biafra wasn't happy to leave it there. A single called 'Holiday In Cambodia', an album sleeve for *Plastic Surgery Disasters* which featured an emaciated African child's arm…nothing was beneath the Kennedys' radar. Inevitably bans followed, most notoriously for a penis/arse piece of poster artwork given away with 1985's *Frankenchrist*. By comparison 'Too Drunk To Fuck' seems almost idiotic in its puerility. That didn't stop it getting a ban, though, and you can only assume Biafra was happy to sing a song this stupid for no other pleasure than getting up the noses of the moral majority.

## BEST LINES
"You give me head/It makes it worse/Take out your fuckin' retainer/Put it in your purse/I'm too drunk to fuck/You're too drunk to fuck."

## CAREER CONSEQUENCES
Given the confrontational nature of the band's attitude it's no surprise that it was all over by 1987. You lose your voice if you keep banging on in exactly the same manner for too long. Biafra, however, has had both an active and an actively political recording career.

# CHRIS DE BURGH

## 'Patricia The Stripper'
From *Spanish Train And Other Stories* (A&M, 1976)

## STYLE
Ragtime-style jam full of parping clarinets and roistering bar-room piano.

## THE SORDID DETAILS
This may come as a surprise to those who only know Chris De Burgh for his abominably schmaltzy 'Lady In Red', but there clearly lurks a filthy mind behind the radio-friendly façade. This is an enjoyable little lollop through a tale of Patricia, "the best stripper in town", and how she managed to avoid the long arm of the law back in 1924. Possibly the most incredible entry of all in this book of bawdiness, Chris De Burgh: we salute you. And whoever thought there was a cat in hell's chance of saying that!?

## BEST LINES
"And with a swing of her hips she started to strip/To tremendous applause she took off her drawers/And with a lick of her lips she undid all her clips/Threw it all in the air and everybody stared."

## CAREER CONSEQUENCES
World domination, multi-platinum sellers by the truckload and that bloody record!

# DE LA SOUL

## 'Buddy'
From *3 Feet High And Rising* (Big Life, 1989)

## STYLE
Laid-back jazzy groovery mixed with relaxed hip hop delivery. Sexy
rather than sleazy, until things get a bit hog-wild at the end.

## THE SORDID DETAILS
While there's no doubt that De La Soul were openly discussing sex on
'Buddy', the feel of the tune is about as far removed from the majority of
flesh-oriented tunes spilling out of the hip hop scene as you can get.
Sitting on the band's astonishing debut album, 'Buddy' was just one
example of a group that was innovative, fun and imaginative, showing
that hip hop could be bent and shaped in a million different directions
while still maintaining its soul and heartbeat. Just one look at the
samples used on the album – including Steely Dan, Johnny Cash, Public
Enemy and Hall & Oates – would be enough to convince even the most
casual listener that here was an act that was born to break the rules.
'Buddy' somehow talks about guys looking for sex in a way which is far
less dick-swinging and far more fun than most rap acts. Hip hop with a
very human touch.

## BEST LINES
**"For the lap Jimbrowski must wear a cap/Just in case the young
girl likes to clap/Ain't for the wind but before I begin/I initiate the
buddy with a slap."**

## CAREER CONSEQUENCES
Never again would the three piece attain the level of success that their
debut offered, but De La Soul are still in effect and still writing
challenging music.

# DIAMOND HEAD

### 'Sucking My Love'
From *Lightning To The Nations* (Fan Club, 1981

##  STYLE
Driving heavy metal from Birmingham, the home of the riff.

##  THE SORDID DETAILS
Diamond Head never made any commercial headway, despite being touted as one of the groups most likely to at the outset of the New Wave Of British Heavy Metal movement at the end of the '70s. However, their legendary status is assured thanks to the constant sponsorship of Metallica drummer Lars Ulrich, a fanatical follower of the band who talked up the Stourbridge four piece at every opportunity. 'Sucking My Love' caused quite a rumpus at the time thanks to its combination of giant riffs and its overt discussion of the pleasures of giving (rather than receiving) oral sex, a novel twist on the self-centred explorations of sex that most metal bands seemed preoccupied with at the time.

##  BEST LINES
"Tasty, tasty, tasty, tasty/Faster...love...make me go/Shoot me/Faster, faster love, sucking my love/Oh Lord, sucking my love/Oh Lord, sucking my love."

##  CAREER CONSEQUENCES
Diamond Head split and reformed on more than one occasion at the behest of Ulrich, but have never achieved any success and will be best remembered for the songs which have been covered by Metallica.

# DIVINYLS

## 'I Touch Myself'
From *Divinyls* (Virgin, 1990)

## STYLE

Gentle, Americanized rock presumably designed to explain the joys of masturbation to intimate gatherings of no more than fifteen thousand. Bring your own lighter.

## THE SORDID DETAILS

Divinyls was the brainchild of Australian duo guitarist Mark McEntee and diva-ish singer Christina Amphlett. Amphlett appeared to be a helpful soul, appearing on the cover of the *Divinyls* album wearing a revealing crochet dress and, frankly, touching herself on her (ample) breast as well as on what would nowadays be referred to as "the poonannie". Nice to see such a literal interpretation of the hit single. Her breathy performance of the song was believed to have been responsible for the awakening of many a junior pocket billiard player. Unfortunately, the rest of the album was of such questionable quality that nobody was inspired to become a diehard Divinyler.

## BEST LINES

"I want you/I don't want anybody else/And when I think about you/I touch myself/Ooh, ooh, oo, oo, aahh."

## CAREER CONSEQUENCES

Created the desired effect of gaining a few column inches. But with nothing else in the locker Divinyls predictably faded into obscurity.

# DJ ASSAULT

## 'Ass'n'Titties'
Single (Assault Rifle, 1996)

## STYLE

What's known as "Booty Music" needs little more in the way of explanation. But if you like things spelling out, imagine electro beats with hardcore porno lyrics. That should just about do it.

## THE SORDID DETAILS

Craig Adams began his DJing career at the tender age of 12 in his hometown of Detroit. His mum and dad were doubtless delighted to think that by 1996 he was seriously hailed in his 'hood for his work alongside fellow DJ Assault member Ade' Mainor on the *Straight Up Detroit Shit* album and the bum and boobs anthem in question. Never designed for the mainstream, 'Ass'n'Titties' nonetheless became an anthem of choice for those with a serious appreciation of, well, ass and titties.

## BEST LINES

"Ass'n'titties, ass'n'titties, ass, ass, titties, titties ass'n'titties."

## CAREER CONSEQUENCES

Never recording with the express intention of topping the *Billboard* charts, our two intrepid heroes dissolved their partnership in 2000, only for Adams to release an album, *Jefferson Avenue*, in 2001 which introduced Assault as a solo artist. Confused? Best not to think about it, really. Just get back to 'Ass'n'Titties', eh?

# THA DOGG POUND

## 'Some Bomb Azz Pussy'
From *Dogg Food* (Death Row, 1995)

## ⊠ STYLE

Sleazy, mucky, mess-all-over the carpet laid-back gangsta rap from the triple header vocal team of Snoop Dogg, Kurupt and Dat Nigga Daz.

## ⊠ THE SORDID DETAILS

Daz and Kurupt had originally made their Death Row reputations as writers and rappers on two seminal hip hop albums, Dre's *The Chronic* and Snoop's *Doggy Style*. On the back of their success came the exploitationally-named Tha Dogg Pound. Boasting exactly the same spooky West Coast sound as Dre and Snoop three years after *The Chronic*, the album wasn't rated as highly as its forerunners, but there's no doubt that it more than punched its weight in terms of sheer unadulterated crudity. 'Some Bomb Azz Pussy' is a tune that makes no attempt to hide its intentions, which is to show all the listeners not how much pussy Daz, Kurupt and guest Snoop get, but how much they get together. And, of course, how exceptional that pussy is.

## ⊠ BEST LINES

"Nigga, where the carat, nigga?/Tear that ass up, yeah, honey, you like that, uh?/Oh yeah, huh, oh, bust a nut, hold it, hold it/Oh, I'm a bust a nut in your motherfuckin' mouth/Hold on, take this motherfucker/(Ooooh, my pussy)/What the fuck then? I'm a bust that in your motherfucker."

## ⊠ CAREER CONSEQUENCES

As the phrase goes: "The people have spoken…the bastards." Voting with their wallets, rap fans gave a big thumbs down to Daz and Kurupt and despite additional solo work neither artists made the grade. Kurupt finally reappeared on Dre's 2001 album.

# LONNIE DONEGAN

## 'Diggin' My Potatoes'
Single (1954, Decca)

## STYLE
Groovy, rootsy, rootin'-tootin' tune that brought real passion and energy to '50s guitar music. That kazoo sound's a bit mad, though.

## THE SORDID DETAILS
Lonnie Donegan single-handedly invented the skiffle sound, an energetic interpretation of the American blues, country and bluegrass sound that the Scot had picked up while working in jazz bands. A single titled 'Rock Island Line', recorded as part of a Chris Barber Jazz Band album, was released and caught fire, selling three million copies worldwide. It was teenagers who really took to Donegan's energetic sound, and they liked him all the more when his 'Diggin' My Potatoes' single was banned on the grounds that the words were too suggestive (which they were). Donegan knew he was on to something and the money started rolling right on in…

## BEST LINES
"Well I tipped up to her window/Wished I had a gun/Mine was wrapped around him/Sure was going some/Man you've been diggin' my potatoes/Trampling on my vine."

## CAREER CONSEQUENCES
Donegan racked up hits galore, influenced the likes of Tommy Steele and Cliff Richard to form skiffle groups and eventually ended up as a producer of some note as well as a performer. He never saw a penny in royalties for 'Rock Island Line' though.

# THE DOORS

**'The End'**
From *The Doors* (Elektra, 1967)

## STYLE

Psychedelic fuzzed-up rock dominated by the keyboards of Ray
Manzarek and Jim Morrison's eerily apocalyptic singing.

## THE SORDID DETAILS

When it first emerged in 1968 The Doors' first album would have
unsettled the establishment with its sound alone. Weird, threatening,
twisted and beautiful, *The Doors* felt confrontational before you'd even
paid attention to what Morrison was singing about. And when you did,
well, how about an eleven-and-a-half-minute song about the Oedipus
Complex to be getting on with? Not the usual "boy meets girl" kind of
deal, Morrison's rap of "Father? I want to kill you. Mother? I want to…"
followed by the most amazing primal scream on record left no-one in
any doubt about which particular taboo the singer was facing up to here.
An astonishing way to end a debut album by anybody's standards.

## BEST LINES

"The killer awoke before dawn/He put his boots on/He took a face
from the ancient gallery/And he walked on down the hall/He went
to the room where his sister lived/And then he paid a visit to his
brother/And then he walked on down the hall/And he came to a
door, and he looked inside/"Father?" "Yes, son?" "I want to kill
you/Mother, I want to…"

## CAREER CONSEQUENCES

Fame, notoriety, arrest for supposedly unleashing his wanger onstage,
death in a bath tub in Paris at the age of 27…Jim Morrison certainly
packed some living into his short time. Career? Did he ever really think
of The Doors as a career?

# DRIVE-BY TRUCKERS

'Too Much Sex (Too Little Jesus)'
From *Pizza Deliverance* (Ghost Meat, 1999)

## STYLE

Southern rock in feel, though there's no electric guitar here, only gravelly vocals and tight-as-a-drum playing.

## THE SORDID DETAILS

This is a wry and clever look at those horrendous evangelists with their slick smiles and even slicker presentation, all designed to wrestle your bucks out of your jeans by preying on your conscience. Stacy is "a troubled teen" trying to make sense of things who is suckered by the smooth tone of a radio station preacher. And while the song contains enough rude words to make a bouncer blush, the point of the tune is a sound one: namely, who exactly is preying on the weak in our society? A dirty song with a conscience — and you don't find too many of them around.

## BEST LINES

"Stop that dope smoking, stop that masturbation!/Take the Lord into your heart and stop that fornication/We're building us an army, gonna knock out Satan/Visa or Mastercard our operators are waiting!/Too much sex, too little Jesus/Too much sex, too little Jesus./Too much sex, too little Jesus."

## CAREER CONSEQUENCES

This lot look like they enjoy stirrings things up deliberately. Their latest effort, *Southern Rock Opera* is a twenty-track double concept album using the tragedy of Lynyrd Skynyrd to examine the concept of Southern heritage. No, really!

# IAN DURY AND THE BLOCKHEADS

## 'Billericay Dickie'
From *New Boots And Panties* (Stiff, 1977)

##  STYLE

Charming jazzy grooves counterpointing cheeky but clever lyrics in a song that was curiously labelled new wave on its release.

## THE SORDID DETAILS

Dury managed to mangle up sex with humour in a way that few have managed before or emulated since. Nowhere was this better displayed than on his tour de force *New Boots And Panties* and 'Billericay...' in particular. For a polio-stricken 35-year-old to be fronting a jazz-playing punk band should have hinted that Dury was not going to be ploughing a traditional furrow. Still, everyone could relate to the theme of the nice bit of rough getting his end away with a variety of different birds and Dury's "glint in the eye" delivery made people warm to his cheekiness, rather than take umbrage at it.

## BEST LINES

"I know a lovely old toe-rag obliging and noblesse/Kindly, charming shag from Shoeburyness/My given name is Dickie, I come from Billericay/I thought you'd never guess."

## CAREER CONSEQUENCES

Dury never again scaled the heights of his early successes, but he always retained a loyal following, as well as generating a lot of warmth and affection from the general public. Broadening his creative talents to include acting, (he appeared in Peter Greenaway's *The Cook, The Thief, His Wife And Her Lover*) Dury remained active until his death from cancer in 2000.

 **DWARVES**

**'Let's Fuck'**
From *Blood, Guts And Pussy* (Sub Pop, 1990)

## STYLE

Fast, furious and quite possibly futile punk thrashing with the added bonus of some girl (possibly an actress) orgasming in the background.

## THE SORDID DETAILS

Chicago garage punks with a taste for the shocking, Dwarves' first release appeared in 1986, but they didn't hit their "creative" stride until *Blood Guts And Pussy*, fourteen minutes of obscene diatribe littered with the word "fuck" and sleeved in a handy "Does Exactly What It Says On The Tin" cover of three naked women covered in animal blood. It's funny for at least five seconds. Dwarves enjoyed the odd wind-up, even press-releasing a story claiming that guitarist He Who Cannot Be Named had died. He hadn't, but the band's label weren't amused and promptly dropped them. Of course this now appears somewhat ironic in the light of what Sub Pop had actually been prepared to release by the band.

## BEST LINES

"I'm made of rubber, you're made of glue/I wanna stick my fucking cock inside of you/Let's fuck/I am the best fuckin' fuck in the whole USA/I can fuck you to death, I can fuck you to stay."

## CAREER CONSEQUENCES

Dumb punks don't disappear, they mutate and survive. 2000's *The Dwarves Come Clean* featured a mix of pop punk and industrial metal. Perhaps more importantly, it featured two naked women covered in soap bubbles on its sleeve.

# EAST 17

'Deep'
From *Walthamstow* (London, 1993)

## STYLE

Groove-oriented dance pop with a sophisticated sheen that ran decidedly counter to the band's oiky image.

## THE SORDID DETAILS

God-bothering vocalist and songwriter Tony Mortimer fashioned a pretty decent career on the back of some half-decent tunes fronted up by three herberty-looking youths. Backed by the muscle of pop impresario Tom Watkins, East 17 touched a nerve with very young fans who didn't want their idols to be as saccharine-sweet as Take That. The combination of youthful yobbery and sex-focused tenderness worked a charm on 'Deep', a song that was clearly about oral sex, but which was delivered in such a way that the youngsters didn't find the insinuation dirty, but rather exciting.

## BEST LINES

"I'm gonna kiss ya from ya head 2 ya toes and then/I'm gonna lick ya where you'd love me to go, yeah!/Oil ya skin within, hold ya tight/Yeah, I'll butter the toast if U lick the knife."

## CAREER CONSEQUENCES

East 17 stayed on top of their game for most of the '90s until Brian Harvey's apparent on-air radio endorsement of ecstasy exposed cracks in the band. His on-off relationship with TV personality and reformed cocaine fiend Daniella Westbrook served only to highlight the differences as Mortimer moved to an even more serene plane. Disintegration was inevitable.

# E-40

## 'Keep Pimpin'
From *Tha Hall Of Game* (Jive, 1996)

### STYLE

Indefinable quirky rap that relies on quick-fire delivery, unfathomable slang and hi-speed switches in vocal style.

### THE SORDID DETAILS

Oakland's Earl Stevens stood up for the profession of pimping on his third album and felt no compunction in hailing it a job of repute. The caring, sharing side of the men who run the whores is brought to the fore as E-40 extols some of their virtues. Hell, they take those girls from giving out for nothing to making a (dis)honest living out of their carnal desires. What top guys they are, one and all!

### BEST LINES

"Man you'd be surprised how many niggaz love to pay for pussy/Niggaz cheat on they wives and jack up all they fuckin' money man/I be givin' my hoes bonuses and benefits/Boat cruises and Kamal outfits/Latex to keep their health a good/Check-ups at Planned Parenthood."

### CAREER CONSEQUENCES

Never made the mainstream, but it wasn't the lyrics that stopped him — let's face it, there are plenty of multi-platinum rappers saying worse. Trouble is, they're saying it more conventionally than E-40 ever did. His rapping style was never going to appeal to the wiggas!

# EMINEM

### 'My Name Is...'
From *The Slim Shady* LP (Interscope, 1999)

## X STYLE

You don't really need this book to tell you. But...ultra-original rap artist whose genius has almost been buried under the reams of press generated since 1999. A fat bass, weasly synth lines and snapping drum groove. But that really isn't the half of it... Indescribable.

## X THE SORDID DETAILS

Listening back to this first track proper from Eminem's first major album proper is still an incredible experience. White boy rap that doesn't ape or imitate, but innovates. Lyrics that are offensive if you don't understand that they're written by a man who is as caustic and cynical as they come. And they say Americans don't understand irony. Sex is a part of Eminem's world, but like everything else it's twisted out of the normal one-dimensional field and suddenly becomes something else entirely. Though who knows what exactly? A truly original, disturbing artist.

## X BEST LINES

"My brain's dead weight, I'm tryin' to get my head straight/But I can't figure out which Spice Girl I wanna impregnate." *(And this from a song that talks about ripping Pamela Lee's tits off!)*

## X CAREER CONSEQUENCES

Moral outrage, column inches, law suits from your mum, multi-platinum success, madness, more column inches. This won't be the end of it.

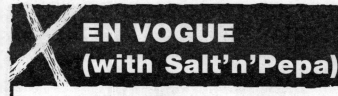

# EN VOGUE
# (with Salt'n'Pepa)

### 'Whatta Man'
From *Funky Divas* (EastWest, 1993)

## STYLE
Strong and sexy R'n'B rap crossover from a tag team combination of six sassy divas.

## THE SORDID DETAILS
Whoever brought together the R'n'B divas En Vogue with the female hip hop trio Salt'n'Pepa clearly knew their onions. Both outfits had the same attitude – strong, sexy, man-loving rather than hating, not prepared to be messed around – and styles which could be blended to perfection. 'Whatta Man' was perfect, a song praising one man in particular, while effectively airing a wish list of what women want. Given that the single was a major hit it's a wonder that no-one picked on the line about the failure of so many to find a woman's clitoris in bed. Pretty rude, but pretty clever at one and the same time.

## BEST LINES
"Yes my man says he loves me/Never says he loves me not/Tryin' a rush me good and touch me in the right spot/See other guys that I've had they tried to play all that Mac shit/But every time they tried I said that's not it."

## CAREER CONSEQUENCES
*Funky Divas* established the band as one of the most influential girl groups of modern times and into the new decade they're still recording.

# MARIANNE FAITHFULL

### 'Why D'Ya Do It?'
From *Broken English* (Island, 1979)

## STYLE

Reggae/rock combination feel that backs a gritty, unflinching look at the pain felt by someone on the sharp end of a partner's infidelity.

## THE SORDID DETAILS

Having been known more for her dalliance with Mick Jagger and that apocryphal Mars bar story, Faithfull suddenly burst into creative life in 1979 with a brutally honest examination of relationship problems. Delivered in a cracked, croaky and deep voice, 'Why D'Ya Do It?' asks the fundamental question of an unfaithful lover, wrenching every last drop of anger, bitterness and despair out of a lyric made all the more emotive because of Faithfull's metamorphosis from angelic beauty to damaged thirty-something. Not for Faithfull, though, the role of subservience in the face of conjugal disaster. This lady is seriously pissed off and she's not going to take this lying down (if you see what I mean!).

## BEST LINES

"Why d'ya do it, she screamed, after all we've said?/Every time I see your dick I see her cunt in my bed."

## CAREER CONSEQUENCES

Sort of stalled, really. Despite numerous releases Faithfull has never scaled any commercial heights, though the suspicion remains that she's never really craved it either. *Broken English* remains her tour de force.

# FATBOY SLIM

## 'Fucking In Heaven'
From *You've Come A Long Way Baby* (Skint Records, 1998)

## STYLE
Big, fat and meaty beats that sealed former Housemartin Norman Cook's reincarnation as party-hardy, cut and paste, mix and match DJ supremo Fatboy Slim.

## THE SORDID DETAILS
After "buggering about in Brighton with some feeble hip hop beats" or "refining his style", depending on your perspective, Fatboy Slim finally came good on his third album, *You've Come A Long Way Baby*. A clever mix of attitudinal beats, intelligent sampling and good old pop sensibility, Slim carried his hipper following with him into chartsville, thanks in no small part to the album's prodigious amount of swearing. Nowhere was the mouth-soap needed more than on 'Fucking In Heaven', where the entire song consists of one mantra repeated over a funky trip good enough for James Brown.

## BEST LINES
"Fatboy Slim is fucking in heaven." *(Repeated ad nauseam.)*

## CAREER CONSEQUENCES
It appears that swearing actually is big and clever. *You've Come A Long Way Baby* became a monstrous hit and Cook married TV babe Zoe Ball. It's not known what new father-in-law, squeaky-clean kiddies TV presenter Johnny Ball, makes of it all.

# THE FLAMING LIPS

## 'Oh My Pregnant Head (Labia In The Sunlight)'
From *Transmissions From The Satellite Heart* (Warner Brothers, 1993)

## STYLE

Dreamy pop touched by the delicate hand of psychedelia with a couple of very, very big powerchords tossed in for luck.

## THE SORDID DETAILS

If there's another song out there in the great pantheon of music that mentions the word "labia" in the title, then I've yet to hear it. Mind you, this isn't such a bizarre thing for a band who have such catchy titles as 'Pilot Can At The Queer Of God' and 'This Here Giraffe' in their armoury. The Oklahoma City outfit, led by Wayne Coyne, has had one of the more colourful rock existences, with members leaving to go on spiritual journeys, almost having their hands amputated and thinking it would be a good idea to record forty cars with their tape decks playing specially composed music. Compared to that little lot, what's the word "labia" in the title of a song? Doesn't amount to a hill of beans does it, really?

## BEST LINES

"Somewhere the star burns the universe/Gold eagle paints in my fingers (all day)/Can of spaghetti diseases/Hopin' that you can still play guitar?/Just like a baby/Just like the smoke rings/Labia in the sunlight." *(Well, glad he's cleared that one up, then!)*

## CAREER CONSEQUENCES

They're still hanging in there. Latest album *Yoshimi Battles The Pink Robots* confirms that The Lips are still clearly doolally. But we wouldn't have them any other way, would we?

# GEORGE FORMBY

### 'With My Little Ukulele In My Hand'
From *Formby On Film, Volume 2* (Sounds On CD, 1985)

## STYLE
English music hall classic with Lancashire's favourite son showing off his chops on his chosen instrument.

## THE SORDID DETAILS
Joe Brown And The Bruvvers had their version of the tune banned in 1963 on the grounds that it was too risqué – and even the most cursory listen to the lyrics will convince you as to why. Formby may have looked like butter wouldn't melt in his mouth, but the double entendre is laid on with a trowel here so that surely even the most naïve and innocent must have thought something was going on. Not only does our George get passionate in the sand with a girl while keeping his hand on his instrument, but he also realises later in the song that his wife's had a baby boy because he too has his ukulele in his hand. You don't have to be Poirot to work it out, do you?

## BEST LINES
"Out of the bedroom door he looked and smiled/Said come inside and see your wife and child/My heart it jumped with joy, I could see it was a boy/For he had a ukulele in his hand."

## CAREER CONSEQUENCES
Big Time Charlie! In the late '30s Formby was Britain's biggest star, earning a whopping £100,000 a year. That'd be enough to make anyone reach for their ukulele and give it a strum!

# FRANKIE GOES TO HOLLYWOOD

### 'Relax'
From *Welcome To The Pleasure Dome* (ZTT, 1984)

## STYLE

Super-camp hi-energy dance with a surprisingly muscular undertow. Trevor Horn's bombastic production obviously had a lot to do with it.

## THE SORDID DETAILS

Frankie's overt flaunting of their fetish-flavoured dancer Paul Rutherford first gained the Liverpool five-piece notoriety in the early '80s, but it was the banning by the BBC of both the video for 'Relax' and subsequently the song itself that led to instant stardom. The video in question featured some folk dressed in leather – tame by today's standards, but it did the trick. And singer Holly Johnson's ultra camp style could be seen to have been brave for the time. The song itself still stands up. Perceived wisdom has it that the tune had been crafted much more by the producer than by the band. But frankly, who cares?

## BEST LINES

"Relax, don't do it/When you wanna come."

## CAREER CONSEQUENCES

Frankie were a flash in the pan and by the time their second album, *Liverpool*, was released in 1986 people had already tired of their lack of substance. Johnson and Rutherford subsequently attempted to launch solo careers.

# THE FUGS

## 'Boobs A Lot'
From *The Fugs First Album* (Fantasy, 1965)

## STYLE
Daft jug-style call and response song that no doubt sounds amazing with a bellyful of moonshine.

## THE SORDID DETAILS
Formed in the Peace Eye bookshop in New York's East Village in 1964, The Fugs could certainly claim to be the first underground rock band – the spiritual precursors of The Mothers Of Invention and The Velvet Underground. Their rudimentary skills didn't hamper their attempt to produce highly political and often highly sexual content – a combination which may seem weird these days, but which made perfect sense at the time. 'Boobs A Lot' is a fun poke at jock mentality, focussing on a group of American footballers and their breast obsession. Gentle, funny and rude.

## BEST LINES
"Down in the locker room, just the boys/Do you wear your jock a lot?/Gotta wear your jock a lot/Do you like boobs a lot?/Gotta like boobs a lot/If you like boobs a lot tag-a-long/If you have a long flagon on..."

## CAREER CONSEQUENCES
This wasn't a group that was built to last and after six relatively successful years of hectoring and madness the band broke up, though The Fugs would come together for periodic reunions over the following years.

# FUNKDOOBIEST

## 'Pussy Ain't Shit'
From *Brothas Doobie* (Epic, 1995)

## STYLE

Mid-tempo hip hoppery driven along against what sounds like a deep sampled bassoon lick. Honestly!

## THE SORDID DETAILS

Latino hip hop with the hand of Cypress Hill's DJ Muggs on the production tiller, Son Doobiest and DJ Ralph M caused some waves with their debut album *Which Doobie U Be* back in 1993. 'Pussy Ain't Shit', from the band's second release, is a 360-degree twist on the usual rap bragging about how much pussy so-and-so can get a hold of. This time the band try to affect an air of total nonchalance toward it, claiming that it's firstly unsanitary and ultimately uninteresting. It's certainly an interesting take on the number one subject that occupies most rappers' minds, but the language chosen to express it is every bit as filthy as anything used by the pro-pussy brigade.

## BEST LINES

"She grabbed my dick with the pussy lips sagging/I just fuck the pussy, then I just throw it out/It ain't shit, the bitches be acting like it's gold."

## CAREER CONSEQUENCES

Never quite made the breakthrough many felt they deserved. If they'd been a little nicer to the ladies and their private parts do you think it could have helped?

# GINGER

## 'Cars And Vaginas'
Single (Infernal Records, 2001)

## STYLE
Retread of classic glam rock sound of the '70s complete with sax parping. Now with added rude words.

## THE SORDID DETAILS
Ginger, frontman of almost-made-the-big-time rock band The Wildhearts, is a prolific writer, who records solo singles in his spare time and flogs them through a singles club to die-hard followers, of which there are a not an inconsiderable amount. 'Cars And Vaginas' is single number two from a proposed "Twelve releases in a year" project and is an ode to the two prime motivators in life for Californian males. And while the song had real commercial friendliness thanks to its T-Rexian pretensions, the chances of a single with the words "cars and vaginas" repeated over and over again ever bruising the charts was something less than nil. Destined always to be a collectors' curio.

## BEST LINES
"So come over here with your chicks and your beer/cars and vaginas/cars and vaginas/cars and vaginas/cars and vaginas/California dreamin', California dreamin', yeah great, good for California."

## CAREER CONSEQUENCES
Ginger has made a career from not worrying about his career. Singles liberally doused in swear words, breaking up bands at the height of success, losing his mind at inappropriate moments, it's all been done and then done again. Ginger is like a weed. No matter how often he's hacked down he always springs up again.

# GLUECIFER

## 'Dick Disguised As Pussy'
From *Head To Head Boredom* (Devil's Doll, 1999)

## STYLE
Thrashing punk rock with a rock'n'roll attitude.

## THE SORDID DETAILS
Norwegian rock doesn't have a long and glamorous history, but if Oslo's Gluecifer are anything to go by, at least they have a sense of humour as well as a foot on the monitor. This is hard rocking punk at its most corrosive, with vocalist Biff Malibu giving it his best possible Iggy-On-Acid impressions. 'Dick Disguised As Pussy' is your regular old tale of transvestite confusion as far as I can tell, though the clarity of diction from friend Biff leaves something to be desired, so that might be made up. On title alone, though, Gluecifer are well worthy of inclusion. And what about that name?!

## BEST LINES
"Those guys/Those guys/Was dick disguised as pussy."

## CAREER CONSEQUENCES
Gluecifer have not as yet managed to make it to the top of the *Billboard* charts. But we live in hope, of course.

# GUNS N'ROSES

## 'Anything Goes'
From *Appetite For Destruction* (Geffen, 1987)

## STYLE
Sleazy rock manufactured out of too many nights spent with lowlifes, junkies and hookers down on Hollywood's Sunset Strip.

## THE SORDID DETAILS
Guns N'Roses made no secret of their scumbag credentials, glorifying in the sex and drugs excesses of the traditional rock'n'roll lifestyle and writing songs about the subject matter they knew with an honesty that was actually a welcome relief to the airbrushed rock poncery of '80s metal. 'Anything Goes' was, frankly, one of the few fillers on their ground-breaking *Appetite For Destruction* album, but it set the tone for the attitude that so captured people's imaginations and which led to superstar status. In an age that was still heavily AIDS-conscious, tales of careless sex were rightly seen as dangerous and exciting.

## BEST LINES
"Panties round your knees with your ass in debris/Doin' dat grind with a push and a squeeze/Tied up, tied down, up against the wall/Be my Rubbermaid baby/An' we can do it all."

## CAREER CONSEQUENCES
Not since Hugh Hefner has filth proved so financially rewarding. Guns N'Roses became one of music's highest-ever grossers through their own undeniable grossness. Great albums, inter-band fighting, drug and girlfriend troubles, artistic tantrums…you got everything and more from Guns N'Roses before they self-destructed in a plume of acrimony. Just as it should be, then.

# HAPPY MONDAYS

## 'Kinky Afro'
From *Pills 'n' Thrills And Bellyaches* (Factory, 1990)

##  STYLE
Drug-addled eccentric pop that defined the whole of the Manchester music revolution in one four minute stab.

##  THE SORDID DETAILS
Where to start? Happy Mondays were always the Stones to the Stone Roses' Beatles in the Madchester scene. Whereas Ian Brown's mob specialised in straight pop melodies, the Mondays were of an altogether rougher sound and character. Led by lunatic vocalist Shaun Ryder's narc-inspired vision of dole, drugs and dicking around, they wrote worldly songs with an other-wordly feel. Like real-life drug addicts, The Mondays could rarely get it up to talk about shagging in their music, but 'Kinky Afro' is, and will always remain, a supremely smutty song purely because of its astonishingly grimy opening line. In many ways it's far more filthy than any stream of horizontally-oriented lyrics you may care to mention.

##  BEST LINES
"Son, I'm 30/I only went with your mother 'cause she's dirty/And I don't have a decent bone in me/What you get is just what you see yeah."

##  CAREER CONSEQUENCES
From the height of his powers when Happy Mondays ruled as The Kings Of Manchester to writing dumb-assed columns for national newspapers, it's been a strange old ride for Shaun Ryder. Black Grape came and went, The Happy Mondays reformed, but nothing will match the buzz of those early "couldn't give a fuck" days.

# HARD-ONS

## 'Suck 'n' Swallow'
From *Dateless Dudes Club* (Waterfront, 1992)

## STYLE
Feedback-heavy, drum-fill heavy, just all-round heavy punk/metal crossover.

## THE SORDID DETAILS
Sydney punks who've been at it since 1980, putting out album after album of deliberately stupid energised surf rock. Dumb as you please and with no aspirations toward art, Hard-Ons have nothing to say and all day to say it, which is a fine state of affairs for those who like to believe musicians are not there to give political insight, but should rather talk about the eternal problem of trying to get sex from girls. If that's you, this band is probably already known to you. And 'Suck 'n' Swallow' isn't about boiled sweets, in case you were wondering.

## BEST LINES
"Suck/Swallow/Suck/Swallow." *(Get the picture?)*

## CAREER CONSEQUENCES
It looked all over for Hard-Ons when there was musical silence following 1993's *Too Far Gone*. But 2001 saw a new album, *This Terrible Place*, and a rise once more for Hard-Ons (sorry about the lame pun).

# PJ HARVEY

**'Rid Of Me'**
From *Rid Of Me* (Island, 1993)

## STYLE

Stealthy and spooky rock that sounds like a Bunny Boiler got hold of a guitar.

## THE SORDID DETAILS

It's the sheer weird pervertedness of this one that means it makes the cut. When she first emerged on to the scene, a scraggy-looking waif with a very big guitar, Polly Harvey split the vote between those who saw her as a crusader reclaiming rock from male dominance and those who thought she was a tuneless pretender. Whatever the merits of her music, though, the idea of a girl who didn't conform to any of the usual sexually provocative stereotypes while still being sexually appealing certainly set tongues wagging. And while some folks might have been put off licking her legs by the idea that she looked like she didn't shave them too often, others were clearly smitten. Different strokes for different folks, as the saying goes.

## BEST LINES

"Lick my legs I'm on fire/Lick my legs of desire/Lick my legs I'm on fire/Lick my legs of desire."

## CAREER CONSEQUENCES

Miss Harvey went from strength to strength, always creating challenging music, always moving her image along, never doing the obvious. Still wouldn't fancy licking her legs, though.

# RICHARD HELL AND THE VOIDOIDS

### 'Love Comes In Spurts'
From *Blank Generation* (Stiff, 1976)

## STYLE

New York punk, which means less of the driving guitars associated with the London scene and more of the arty pretensions as espoused by Patti Smith.

## THE SORDID DETAILS

Richard Meyers was one of the founder members of the New York scene of the mid-'70s together with his friend Tom Miller (soon to become Tom Verlaine), having relocated to the city from Lexington, Kentucky. His nihilistic view of life on *Blank Generation* perfectly suited the mood of the times, though 'Love Comes In Spurts' is a song with a twist in the tale. While clearly designed to lull the reader into the belief that what we're dealing with here is the ecstasy of ejaculation, the lyrics are actually disappointingly winsome, dealing with the trauma induced by sudden bouts of lovesickness. So why's it featured in a rude records round-up? Because with a title like that it'd be rude not to.

## BEST LINES

"Love comes in spurts (oh no it hurts)/Love comes in spurts (it hurts)/Love comes in spurts (oh no, cuz)/Love comes in spurts (it always hurts)."

## CAREER CONSEQUENCES

Hell never scaled any great commercial heights, but has managed to carve himself an interestingly creative career as an actor, novelist, poet and sometime musician. Of course the discerning culture vultures among us will also be aware of his finest role – Madonna's boyfriend in the 1985 film *Desperately Seeking Susan*.

# THE HEPTONES

### 'Fattie Fattie'
Single (Studio One, 1966)

## ✖ STYLE
Super smooth rocksteady featuring exquisite and easy harmonies, which runs counter to the lecherous feelings espoused by the tune.

## ✖ THE SORDID DETAILS
This '60s Kingston three piece were so smooth they could surely have charmed the pants off any girl they came across. Leroy Sibbles, Earl Morgan and Barry Llewellyn's first hit is a classic easy reggae groove, made all the more remarkable for its straightforward lyrical message. Their opening gambit of "I need a fat girl/A fat girl tonight/I need a very, very fat girl/A fat girl tonight" won't have the feminists signing up for their love-hungry manifesto. But fat girls would certainly have been impressed by this love of plumptious credentials. If only bogling had been invented at the time the results could have been devastating!

## ✖ BEST LINES
"I'm in the mood, in the mood/I need some food/I'm feeling rude, so rude/When you feel it girl you're gonna say it's so nice."

## ✖ CAREER CONSEQUENCES
The Heptones went on to have an outstanding career and are rightly revered as one of the greatest close harmony groups of all time. Shabba Ranks even did a reworking of 'Fattie Fattie' on his 1995 album *A Mi Shabba*.

# ICE-T

## 'Girls L.G.B.N.A.F.'
From *Power* (Sire, 1988)

## ✕ STYLE

Old school rap complete with ancient-sounding beats, sparse production and the usual bragging, utterly unbothered by any notion of political correctness.

## ✕ THE SORDID DETAILS

Long before the dalliance with heavy metal in Body Count, way before the acting, the TV presenting and the general ubiquitousness of Ice-T in the mainstream media, Tracy Morrow was making music in and for the ghetto. Nothing gets as close to the hedonistic knuckle as 'Let's Get Butt Naked And Fuck', a paean to the power of the penis in T's pants. It's just your regular bout of rap bragging about snagging girls and having sex – crass but ultimately unthreatening. And interestingly enough, even in among all the groin-thrusting stuff Ice T's social conscience still makes an appearance with a warning about the threat of AIDS, proving that even at his most carnal, there was always something going on up top with Ice-T.

## ✕ BEST LINES

**"I only speak what's true/You say you don't, but I know you do/Come on up to my room/We'll undress by the light of the moon/Lay down and I'll caress that butt/Girl, Let's Get Butt Naked And Fuck!"**

## ✕ CAREER CONSEQUENCES

Still one of the true stars to have emerged from the rap scene, Ice-T may have alienated those who first took him to their hearts, but they've been replaced by a more mainstream audience who see Ice-T as the intelligent (and possibly unthreatening) face of hip hop.

# THE ISLEY BROTHERS

## 'Between The Sheets'
From *Between The Sheets* (Epic, 1983)

## STYLE
A super-sassy groove with a vocal delivery pitched halfway between romanticism and lasciviousness.

## THE SORDID DETAILS
One of the greatest of all vocal groups whose fifty-year career has seen two generations of siblings involved in the dynasty. Among the hundreds of songs the band have recorded and the dozens of hits they've had nestles 'Between The Sheets', a 1983 tune that plays at a tempo that puts it somewhere just above ballad, possibly due to the more graphic than romantic nature of the lyrics. Leaving nothing to the imagination, Ronald Isley gives his usual soulful performance as he gets down to business with his chosen lady. Given that his brother Rudolph was later to join the ministry it's unlikely he would have been letting too many copies of this particular release into his church.

# BEST LINES
"Oh, I like the way you receive me (Receive me, receive me)/Girl, I love the way you relieve me/I'm comin' on, comin' on strong (Comin' on strong)/Sweet darlin' in between the sheets."

## CAREER CONSEQUENCES
It appears that none of fire, rain, flood or pestilence can stop The Isleys and they continue to be revered as one of the greatest and most enduring groups of our times.

# JACKYL

## 'She Loves My Cock'
From *Jackyl* (Geffen, 1992)

## STYLE

Idiot-encouraging '90s metal inspired by sex, partying, booze, loud music and the US Treasury's innovative monetary policies. (One of these inspirations is not strictly true.)

## THE SORDID DETAILS

Jackyl were every redneck's dream. Led by vocalist Jesse James Dupree, a man whose stage speciality was bringing out a chainsaw and then "playing" a solo on it, and featuring a guitarist named Jimmy Stiff (apparently not a reference to his guitar style!), they were the very definition of knuckleheadedness. "If you don't have a sense of humour, take this record back...and buy a Perry Como album," said Dupree of his debut effort and proceeded to tickle all funny bones with 'She Loves My Cock'. What this paean to the penis lacked in subtlety it attempted to make up for in sheer exuberance. Unfortunately, it was absolutely bloody awful.

## BEST LINES

"She loves my cock/She loves my cock/She loves my cock/She loves my cock."

## CAREER CONSEQUENCES

Bearing in mind that this gumbylicious album was released in the same year as Nirvana's *Nevermind*, it's no surprise that Jackyl's trajectory was ultimately downward. However, full marks for effort. Jackyl were last heard of waving the American flag with 'Open Invitation', an anti-Osama Bin Laden song, believe it or not. Sample lines? "I'm pissed off and not a patient man/I'd drop a bomb on Afghanistan/I'd snatch that towel from round your head/Wrap it round your neck." Gosh!

# JAM PONY EXPRESS

'Lick It Down'
From *The Legend Continues* (Express, 1995)

##  STYLE

Hardcore dance/rap crossover taken at breakneck speed with harder than average beats.

## STYLE THE SORDID DETAILS

If there's a man out there who's not prepared to get down on his hands and knees for a lady after hearing this four minutes of pure sex (and we're even including Italian mafiosa here) then there is something seriously wrong with him. This is an addictive hardcore dance tune that burns along at a furious pace with a hard hitting female vocal imploring men to get with the zen of oral sex. It would be rude not to after that, wouldn't it?

## BEST LINES

"Boy I hope your tongue is long/Lick it, lick it down/Lick it lick it down."

## CAREER CONSEQUENCES

It appears the Express went into retreat after '95. But judging by the shape of the booty on the cover of *The Legend Continues* one can only assume they were too preoccupied to bother with making music.

# JA RULE

## 'The Murderers'
From *Venni, Vetti, Vecci* (Def Jam, 1999)

## STYLE
Hardcore rap delivered with the kind of mean voice that can scare prison inmates.

## THE SORDID DETAILS
Even before he launched his solo career Ja Rule was forging a bad boy reputation, contributing a verse to Jay Z's 'Can I Get A…' which went on to be a huge hit in 1998. When Jeffrey Atkins' solo career got underway with *Venni, Vetti, Vecci* the likelihood was that he'd be another tough and gruff rapper destined to sit undistinguished from all the gangstas out there. It was only with his second album *Rule 3:36* that Ja found his schtick for hits. Duetting with females to produce pop/rap crossovers yielded huge results and the formula was refined on 'Pain Is Love', with both Jennifer Lopez and Ashanti contributing. So you think Ja Rule isn't really gangsta any more? Then check out 'The Murderers' to see he's not always been the happy clappy face of rap.

## BEST LINES
"J the A R.U.L.E. with them hoez get between more sheetz than Isley/You can't deny me, I'm the muthafuckin' one/Druggin bitches like Heron."

## CAREER CONSEQUENCES
All good, once he went MTV cuddly, that is. Tough-talking streetwise rap certainly isn't what Ja's known for these days.

# JODECI

## 'Ride'n'Slide'
From *Diary Of A Mad Band* (Uptown, 1993)

## STYLE

Smooth as chocolate ballad that sounds like it was written to have sex to.

## THE SORDID DETAILS

Jodeci's sweet and soulful harmonies and laid-back style might lead you to believe you're dealing with some nice, quiet boys here, but you'd better think again. Hailing from Charlotte, North Carolina, when the band members originally met a fight almost broke out over some girl or other. Following a major deal and almost instant success, more troubles followed, when members K-Ci and Devante admitted threatening a woman with a gun and fondling her breast. Then Devante's house was robbed while he was held hostage with a gun in his mouth. And if all that doesn't convince you of Jodeci's lowdown credentials then you haven't listened to 'Ride'n'Slide'. These boys make music you just know the ladies love – and doubtless it's helped them into a few pairs of panties in its time. It's what you call loving by stealth...

## BEST LINES

"You can get a ride, I wanna slide tonight baby/I'm gonna hear you moan so right/Sugar feel my tongue move up and down/I can taste the waters streaming down/Girl you taste so fine."

## CAREER CONSEQUENCES

Jodeci are still together and working on an album (their first together since 1995!) which should be released in 2003.

# LIL JOHNSON

## 'Meat Balls'
From *Complete Works in Chronological Order, Vol. 2* (1936-1937) (Document, 1995)

## STYLE
Sleazy and sassy old blues from a sleazy and sassy old blues lady

## THE SORDID DETAILS
An Olympic standard user of the double entendre in her lyrics and the self-styled "Hottest Gal In Town", Lil's good time blues and hokum style really upped the raunch factor wherever she went. Her love of sexual innuendo was even considered too hot for the times and songs such as 'My Baby (Squeeze Me Again)' were deemed too rude for release, only finally appearing on this 1995 collection. Still, tunes like 'If You Can Dish It (I Can Take It)' and 'Press My Button' made it to vinyl, which suggests that Lil's one woman crusade to put the blue into blues wasn't an entire failure. Hats off to Lil too, for putting on record the most food analogies ever for sex and sexual organs, including meat, peanuts and even cabbage! As legacies go, you could do worse!

## BEST LINES
"Someone send me a butcher, he must be long and tall/If he want to grind my meat, 'cos I'm wild about meat balls/He can clean my fish, even pick my crabs/But what I need is my meat ground bad."

## CAREER CONSEQUENCES
Hard to tell. Lil was recording up to 1937, but nobody appears to know what became of her and her saucy ways, more's the pity!

# GRACE JONES

## 'Pull Up To The Bumper'
From *Nightclubbing* (Island, 1981)

##  STYLE

Super slick and smooth funked-up reggae thanks to a Sly and Robbie
production that perfectly complements Jones' robotic delivery.

##  THE SORDID DETAILS

She may be more famous in the UK for attacking former chat show host
Russell Harty and for having a square head, but Grace Jones' one stab at
the big time has proved to be an endearing and enduring song. The
Amazonian Kingstonian Jones may have had an androgynous look about
her, but there was no way that anyone could misinterpret her totally
transparent lyrical double entendres, utilising as it does the traditional
"car as penis" analogy. Nor could its insistent rhythmic drive be ignored
as a song that not only dealt with the subject of sex, but sounded like it
was a record that you should actually be having sex to as well.

##  BEST LINES

"Pull up to the bumper baby/In your long black limousine/Pull up
to the bumper baby/And drive it in between."

##  CAREER CONSEQUENCES

'Pull Up To The Bumper' has overshadowed everything else Jones has
attempted in her musical career and still remains the one classic in her
armoury (even being used in ads for the Toon Disney channel!). Of
course she has appeared in Eddie Murphy's 1992 film classic *Boomerang*,
so it's not as if she hasn't had major success in other parts of the
entertainment business, is it?!

# JUDGE DREAD

### 'Big Eight'
From *Working Class Ero* (Trojan, 1973)

## STYLE

Bizarre interpretation of ska from a large white man who added *Carry On...* style sauce to the beat, made it a smidge ruder, then sat back and let the Moral Majority do the rest.

## THE SORDID DETAILS

Alex Hughes was born in Brixton and first came into contact with Jamaican music as a bouncer in local clubs in the '60s. In 1969 Hughes enjoyed underground success with a dirty song called 'Big Five', an interpretation of Brook Benton's 'Rainy Night In Georgia'. 'Big Six' went to number 11 in 1972, 'Big Seven' followed, but all these cheeky underground hits were as nothing compared to – you guessed it – 'Big Eight', a ludicrous cod-ska effort with Dread delivering some of the weakest sexual innuendos this side of Larry Grayson. No wonder he wanted his records banned. If anyone actually heard them before buying he wouldn't have flogged any.

## BEST LINES

"Pussy pussy where you been/Why you dirty and not clean/It really shocks me to my feet/See pussy dirty when I eat."

## CAREER CONSEQUENCES

The hit singles soon dried up, as you might expect from a novelty artist, but there was much worse news to come for The Judge, who died on stage on Friday March 13, 1998, age 53, at the Penny Theatre in Canterbury. He was halfway through singing one of his classics, 'The Winkle Man', when he died of a heart attack. His final words were "let's hear it for the band". Well, it could have been worse.

# JUNGLE BROTHERS

## 'Jimbrowski'
From *Straight Out The Jungle* (Idler, 1988)

## ◼ STYLE

Sparse, beat-driven hip hop that relies on interest in the lyric rather than any neat musical twists to make it fly.

## ◼ THE SORDID DETAILS

Despite arriving on the hip hop scene with a jazz-influenced style around the same time as De La Soul and A Tribe Called Quest, Jungle Brothers never managed to create a sizeable buzz for their groove – and this despite being part of the Native Tongue Posse, a loose collective formed by the legendary Afrikaa Bambaataa and including Queen Latifah. Counter to their generally over-serious vibe, 'Jimbrowski' is about as throwaway an ode to the Johnson as it's possible to get. Child-like in its approach, the cut beats work their way underneath a rap about the Jimbrowski being "seven foot tall" and something that the little girls shouldn't mess with. In short, it's rude but rubbish.

## ◼ BEST LINES

"Jimbrowski, yeah, that's what they call it/The thing's so big you need a U-haul to haul it."

## ◼ CAREER CONSEQUENCES

Always the bridesmaids and never the brides, Jungle Brothers lived in the considerable shadow of De La Soul's *3 Feet High And Rising* album and haven't ever really recovered.

# KID ROCK

## 'Fuck You Blind'
From *The Polyfuze Method* (Continuum, 1993)

## STYLE

Early incarnation of Kid Rock sees the soon-to-be fuser of hip hop and southern rock experimenting with low-down, lo-fi, keyboard-heavy grooving. Saints preserve us.

## THE SORDID DETAILS

Recorded long before Bob Ritchie hooked up with a major label and went supernova, this is Kid Rock at his most bitter, twisted and misogynistic. While that might not endear him to his new-found party metal fans, anti-social songs like this are the very reason why The Kid has been championed by working class American trailer trash from the off. A sinister P-funk style keyboard riff, clearly synthetic drums and hardly a power chord in sight, nothing about this musical escapade is fully formed, besides the full frontal, middle digit attitudinal lyrics. But it's a curiously appealing record all the same.

## BEST LINES

"I like that long hair swinging in them Calvin Kleins/I pull them young, start fucking with their virgin minds/I give a fuck about your poppa or your mother/I walk among your ass and bitch slap your brother."

## CAREER CONSEQUENCES

Irrelevant really. The Kid was hardly registering a bleep on music's radar when this tune was recorded, so the only effect it may have had on his career is to have got some of his youngest fans grounded by irate mums after they were caught listening to *The History Of Rock*, a compilation of some of the man's early efforts released post supernova trajectory.

# KING MISSILE

### 'Detachable Penis'
From *Happy Hour* (Atlantic, 1992)

## STYLE

Quirky yet catchy tune about the everyday subject matter of having a detachable penis and an absent-minded personality.

## THE SORDID DETAILS

Knowing that this New York band was originally known as King Missile (Dog Fly Religion) might help here. Otherwise how would you guess that King Missile were capable of writing a stream of consciousness piece about losing your dick because it just happens to be detachable? The song actually emerged out of an off-the-cuff joke about the title of the band's next single that vocalist John S Hall made at one of the band's gigs. Of course the irony of it all is that once they'd recorded a song of that name, it went on to become the band's biggest hit, unbelievably with MTV airplay to boot. What's that they say about life imitating art?

## BEST LINES

"I woke up this morning with a bad hangover and my penis was missing again/This happens all the time: it's detachable/This comes in handy a lot of the time/I can leave it home when I think it's going to get me in trouble/Or I can rent it out when I don't need it."

## CAREER CONSEQUENCES

Well it wasn't going to get any better than your detachable penis song actually becoming a hit, now, was it?

# KING SUN

### 'Coming Soon'
From *X-Rap* – Various Artists (K-Tel, 1991)

## STYLE
Groovy Tone Loc-style rap with hot guitar licks for added sleaze effect.

## THE SORDID DETAILS
While he might be best known for his Afro-centric lyrics and fully paid-up membership of The Nation of Islam, that didn't seem to stop King Sun from indulging himself in some full-on hedonism if 'Coming Soon' is anything to go by. No prizes at all for guessing that the title doesn't refer to a man phoning his wife to reassure her after working late. But Sun's flow is surprisingly restrained, dealing as it does with his own nervousness at dating a woman who's 30 when he's by his own admission a naïve 21. Still, all's well that ends well as Sun gets back to this rich woman's apartment (complete with bear skin rug and fireplace, no less!) and gives her the benefit of his inexperience. Judging by the sounds of female orgasm that permeate the end of the record it's a job well done for the young buck.

## BEST LINES
"I'm like Marvin, I need healing/I don't believe it she has a glass ceiling."

## CAREER CONSEQUENCES
With the advent of gangsta rock, raps like these seem remarkably outdated and genteel, which may have something to do with why King Sun hasn't become a household name. Still a good track, though.

# LILLIAN MAE KIRKMAN

**'He's Just My Size'**
From *Raunchy Business: Hot Nuts & Lollypops*
(Columbia/Legacy, 1991)

## STYLE
Risqué and obscure blues number recorded in 1939 in Chicago.

## THE SORDID DETAILS
Not much is known about Lillie Mae, a local singer whose recording career spanned well over a decade. She's believed to have hailed from St Louis, but settled in Chicago and recorded in the late '30s for the Vocalion label. Well known in The Windy City, she appeared regularly throughout the '40s at a place called Martin's Corner on the city's West Side, often backed by the Jump Jackson band. Always ready to lay down a risqué tune, 'He's Just My Size' obviously dealt with her horizontal preoccupations, while 'Hop Head Blues' is a pretty self-explanatory paean to the booze.

## BEST LINES
"I met a man last night was just my size/I taken him home with me to bake my cakes and pies/That man makes my bread rise way late hours of the night/The kind of bread he serves I swear is out of sight."

## CAREER CONSEQUENCES
Billing herself as "The Queen Of The Blues" was an object lesson in bigging yourself up. It appears that Lillie Mae never really made it out of the Chicago clubs.

# KISS

## 'Plaster Caster'
From *Love Gun* (Casablanca, 1977)

##  STYLE

Dumb and none-too-well played but infectious hard rock from the self-styled "Hottest Band In The World" at their fire-breathing, stack-heel wearing, make-up sporting peak.

##  THE SORDID DETAILS

Kiss bassist Gene Simmons, a man with a very big tongue, an enormous black book and an even larger ego, was delighted by the idea of notorious groupie Cynthia Plaster Caster, a lady whose speciality was making plaster casts of the dicks of rock'n'roll's glitterati back in the days before such lewd behaviour had become old hat. Simmons never had his cock immortalised by the good lady, but was so chuffed by her work that he immediately wrote a song about it.

##  BEST LINES

"The plaster's getting harder/And my love is perfection/I'm talking of my love for her collection." (*Incidentally, didn't Simmons miss out on the most obvious rhyming couplet here, given the nature of the song?*)

##  CAREER CONSEQUENCES

Kiss never again scaled the heights of popularity they enjoyed with *Love Gun*, though whether this is confirmation of the appeal of 'Plaster Caster' or of its ability to stop Kiss fans buying their records is open to debate. Simmons' love-making exploits continued unabashed, however, and he even has a colour photo album recording each and every one of the 4,600 women he's done it with. Romantic old fool!

# KITTIE

### 'Get Off (You Can Eat A Dick)'
From *Spit* (Artemis, 1999)

## STYLE
Slow and discordant metal which builds up to…hey, fast and discordant metal.

## THE SORDID DETAILS
This four-piece all-girl act from Ontario seems out to prove that gals can rawk just as hard as boys in the world of metal. If that's the case they've succeeded, for there's no doubting the ferocity of Kittie's music. Where the band don't follow the traditional rock blueprint is in their lyrical content, which is super pro-feminist. Nothing wrong with a bit of self-assertion, of course, but sometimes it's hard to work out exactly what it is that Kittie are ranting against. They're still young and some of their lyrics sound like they could well have been scribbled on the back of their schoolbooks. Hope their parents don't see them, though!

## BEST LINES
"Dog...is you/Rude, vulgar, obsessive, not true/Once in your life you wouldn't be so sure/You can eat a dick! Humiliation, I'm suffocating."

## CAREER CONSEQUENCES
Still batting on though, frankly, with no chance of ever leaving a real mark. Feminism? Just not that commercial in metal terms, is it?

# KOOL KEITH

## 'Girl Would U Fuck Tonight'
From *Sex Style* (Funky Ass, 1997)

### STYLE
Spartan sound based around nothing much more than thick keyboard splurges and the constant noise of a girl orgasming.

### THE SORDID DETAILS
Originally the main man with Bronx-based outfit The Ultramagnetic MCs, Kool Keith stepped out on his own with a variety of solo projects under a number of different names, including Dr Octagon, Rhythm X and Doctor Dooom. In his double K persona, however, our man has only one thing on his mind. This particular track begins with Keith's mate Mark giving him a call just to catch up – and to tell him that he's got a girl licking his bottom on the drum machine. Well, it's nice to share, isn't it? Things get even more mucky from thereon in as KK goes into graphic detail about a clutch of sexual activities, some involving diapers and a toilet bowl. One for the sexually adventurous, it would seem.

### BEST LINES
*(After a whole song of debauchery, KK suddenly gets a conscience in the very last line. Weird.)* "Watch my testicles regurgitate/Fuck your girlfriend, I put fingers in her ass, she like to hate/You trust me, put on your lingerie and have faith/Condom on my dick, let's be safe."

### CAREER CONSEQUENCES
Still at it, Keith's latest venture, KHM, is: "Brand new super space bounce. We're basically an anti-group, very rebel." Super space bounce, huh? That explains it.

# KORN

## 'A.D.I.D.A.S.'
From *Life Is Peachy* (Immortal/Epic, 1996)

## STYLE
Grinding, melody-light nu-metal that sounds like it wants you to believe sex is something to be endured rather than enjoyed.

## THE SORDID DETAILS
Korn vocalist Jonathan Davis was tempted from his life as a mortuary science student by the promise of making dense, angsty, menacing metal music. No surprise, then, that even a song dealing with the life-affirming subject of sex should be a dark and depressing lyrical affair in Korn's hands. Not that rock fans see it that way. Korn's ascent from California wannabes to stadium fillers has been as unrelenting as their music. But metal has clearly come a long way when a song called 'All Day I Dream About Sex' can sound a thousand times more like Killing Joke than Mötley Crüe.

## BEST LINES
"Screaming to be the only way /That I can truly be free from my fucked up reality/So I turn and stroke it harder/ 'Cos it's so fun to see my face staring back at me/I don't know your fucking name/So what, let's fuck."

## CAREER CONSEQUENCES
Korn go from strength to strength, though let's hope they've loosened up a bit by now, eh? Otherwise being a groupie for this lot isn't going to be a bundle of laughs, is it?

# LATEX GENERATION

## 'Fuck Me I'm A Rock Star'
From *360 Degrees* (One Foot, 1996)

## STYLE

Poppy, punky anthems from a band that takes itself really seriously, as evidenced by the fact they do a cover of a song by big-haired rockers Poison.

## THE SORDID DETAILS

A New York State pop punk band who failed to ride the wave of The Offspring and took a wrong turn off the highway somewhere before the arrival of Sum 41 and Blink 182. So what went wrong? Damn, they even had the obligatory number-incorporating alternative spelling of L8X (get it?). Who knows? The only legacy that exists is an entry in a book championing the rudest records of all time. Their mums will be pleased. As will their bank managers.

## BEST LINES

"Fuck me I'm a rock star."

## CAREER CONSEQUENCES

To steal a line from a very old review of a very different band: They went absolutely nowhere. Then backward.

# LED ZEPPELIN

## 'The Lemon Song'
From *Led Zeppelin II* (Atlantic, 1969)

## ✗ STYLE

Multi-tempoed, superannuated blues bluster from the kings of hairy rock.

## ✗ THE SORDID DETAILS

For a group who prided themselves on the bulges in their collective trousers, Led Zeppelin were a surprisingly restrained bunch when it came to talking up their sexual exploits on record. In the time-honoured traditions of the blues artists they so reverentially worshipped, Zeppelin never really went full bore to the core of the action, preferring to leave much of the carnal caper stuff to either the listeners' imaginations or to a set of handy metaphors. 'The Lemon Song' is the most famous of Robert Plant's sexual exhortations, where the Wolverhampton wanderer pleads with the object of his affections to squeeze him "till the juice runs down my leg". Subtle by today's standards, but in 1969 this was still daring stuff, sexual revolution or no sexual revolution.

## ✗ BEST LINES

"Squeeze me baby till the juice runs down my leg/Squeeze me baby till the juice runs down my leg/The way you squeeze my lemon I'm gonna fall right out of bed."

## ✗ CAREER CONSEQUENCES

With global domination achieved quick smart, Zeppelin were then left to terrorise the women of the world, especially North America, inside their silver-nosed, super-phallic tour jet. Tales of red snappers in Seattle surely don't need repeating one more time, especially if you happen to be the receiving groupie!

# JULIA LEE

### 'King Size Poppa'
From *Tonight's The Night* (Charly, 1987)

## STYLE
Big-hearted blues from one of the sassiest ladies representing the style.

## THE SORDID DETAILS
With songs like 'My Sin' and 'Pagan Love Song' in her armoury, jazz singer Julia Lee certainly wasn't backward when it came to putting the sex into her swing. Her lyrical double entendres and rollicking piano style saw her becoming a major star in Kansas City. Starting off playing and singing in her brother George E. Lee's band throughout the '20s and early '30s, it wasn't until 1944 that Julia got her overtly sexual songs on to disc when she signed a recording deal with Capitol. *Julia Lee And Her Boy Friends* was a risky old title for the time! The liaison lasted for six years and resulted in the vast majority of her recorded material.

## BEST LINES
"When he's around there's not a thing I lack/When he loves me he holds nothing back/Everything I need he carries in those king sized pants."

## CAREER CONSEQUENCES
Singing her raunchy numbers paid off for Julia's early Capitol years, but after 1952 Lee recorded just four more songs before her death in 1958.

# LEGS DIAMOND

### 'I Think I Got It'
From *A Diamond Is A Hard Rock* (Phonogram, 1977)

##  STYLE

Stomping hard rock with a melodic ear and more than a cursory nod toward Deep Purple

##  THE SORDID DETAILS

Los Angeles band Legs Diamond received tons of critical support for their swaggering, keyboard-heavy sound, but never made any kind of commercial breakthrough. This, despite opening for Kiss on their 1976 Rock & Roll Over US tour at a time when the painted New Yorkers were the hottest ticket in the world. 'I Think I Got It' adds a clever spin to the time-honoured tale of on-the-road infidelity. While vocalist Rick Sanford was out on tour keeping his hands to himself – so the lyric has it – his girlfriend at home took the opportunity to spread a little love around by getting through "every boy in town". Result? One cheesed off vocalist with a dose of the clap.

##  BEST LINES

"I think I got it/I think I got it from you/I think I got it/I don't know what to do/I think I got it so tell me, tell me the truth/I ain't been fooling round so who's been fooling with you?"

##  CAREER CONSEQUENCES

Legs Diamond are still active to this day. Hopefully, Sanford's little bit of trouser trouble has long since cleared up!

# THE LEMONHEADS

## 'Big Gay Heart'
From *Come On Feel The Lemonheads* (Atlantic, 1994)

## STYLE

Pure country pop from the handsome almost-was leader of the alternative post-grunge scene.

## THE SORDID DETAILS

A rude record based on the incongruous juxtaposition of a beautiful country pop tune guaranteed to be a massive hit, together with a lyric seemingly designed to subvert any chance of mainstream success. As if calling your biggest potential hit 'Big Gay Heart' wasn't weird enough, Evan Dando then proceeded to chuck in the odd fellatio reference just to rub people's noses right in it. His record company must have been delighted. Dando was, by his own admission, a little bit wobbly with drink and drugs at this stage, so this may have had something to do with his decision-making process. Of course, he may just have been a contrary bastard by nature.

## BEST LINES

"Either way you got a bone to pick, can't you leave that to somebody else?/I don't need you to suck my dick or to help me feel good about myself/Big gay heart, please don't break my big gay heart/Big gay heart, please don't break my big gay heart."

## CAREER CONSEQUENCES

Dando never really made the leap into the major league that his talents deserved and looks should have guaranteed. Maybe it was something to do with his bizarre decision to be photographed in bed with Courtney Love wearing a T-shirt emblazoned with the words "Evil Dildo", just as Kurt Cobain blew his head off. He still records, but hasn't become the icon many expected him to be.

# LIL' KIM

## 'Suck My Dick'
From *Notorious K.I.M.* (Atlantic, 2000)

## STYLE
Curious acoustic backdrop and flapping bass drum drives a bizarre tune from the hardcore girl who might possibly not have a problem with telling you that she quite likes sex.

## THE SORDID DETAILS
Having broken through on Junior M.A.F.I.A.'s debut album Conspiracy in 1995, Kim's career was launched in earnest with her own album *Hard Core* in 1996. Mentored by The Notorious B.I.G. and produced by Puff Daddy, Kim made her own name by choosing to out-do the boys on their own "sex and cussin" terrain. *Hard Core* was precisely that: ultra "Parental Advisory" and maybe more shocking because this was a girl talking about her sexual misadventures with as much groin-oriented gusto as her male counterparts. 'Suck My Dick' (as in: "If I was a dude I'd tell ya, 'suck my dick'.") from her follow-up release is, if anything, a harder lyrical attack, featuring rhymes that could make even Dr Dre blush.

## BEST LINES
"Look I ain't tryin' to suck ya/I might not even fuck ya/Just lay me on this bed and give me some head/Got the camcord layin' in the drawer where he can't see/Can't wait to show my girls he sucked the piss out my pussy."

## CAREER CONSEQUENCES
Such outright muckiness only seems to have helped, as the massive hit 'Lady Marmalade', alongside Christina Aguilera, Mya and Pink has proved.

# LIL' LOUIS

## 'French Kiss'
From *French Kiss* (Sony, 1989)

 **STYLE**

Trancey, hypnotic dance groove that clearly had nothing at all to do with drug culture.

 **THE SORDID DETAILS**

If you can get banned by the BBC you know you're doing something right. If you can get banned by the BBC for a track with no words at all, just because they don't like the style of the breathing on it, you know you're doing something extraordinarily right. Chicago house producer Lil' Louis hit the jackpot with this dancey number, where too much heavy breathing was blamed for its omission from the airwaves. Not that Louis Sims would have been remotely bothered by the British ban. 'French Kiss' had already become a worldwide platinum hit and set his career up just peachily.

 **BEST LINES**

"Uuurgh, uurgh, uuurghhh." *(Or something similar.)*

 **CAREER CONSEQUENCES**

After two albums which fused jazz, R'n'B and house, Lil' Louis moved back into production, setting up his own studio in New York and working with Babyface and Me'Shell NdegeOcello among others.

# LITTLE FEAT

**'Rocket In My Pocket'**
From *Waiting For Columbus* (Warner Bros, 1978)

##  STYLE

Gruff old bluesy rock with a sleazy edge designed for those who like
their music rootsy and reefer-headed.

## THE SORDID DETAILS

Led by former Mother Of Invention Lowell George, Little Feat were
always a critics' favourite, but failed to capitalise on such goodwill with
major commercial success. Of course there's no telling how much more
the band would have achieved had it not been for the erratic behaviour
of George, who split the band in 1979, only to die from a heart attack
that same year. Then again, would Little Feat have been such a diverse,
oddball group (combining blues, funk and country) had it not been for
the maverick approach of their leader? 'Rocket In My Pocket' is a pretty
straightforward "horny bloke/unreceptive girl" idea, but the brazen
rhyming couplet alone makes it a song of some considerable sauce.

## BEST LINES

**"The music was hot, but my baby was not/I've got a rocket in my
pocket, I said rocket/Ya fingers in the socket."**

## CAREER CONSEQUENCES

Little Feat reformed in 1988 and have continued to release albums right
up to the present day to mixed critical reaction. For many the band
ended when George pulled the plug.

# LITTLE RICHARD

## 'Good Golly Miss Molly'
From *Little Richard* (RCA Camden, 1958)

## STYLE
No-holds barred rock'n'roll from one of the genre's true originators and showmen.

## THE SORDID DETAILS
Richard Penniman's elevation to the status of rock legend has much to do with his outlandish hairdos, enthusiastic piano-bashing and all-round over-the-top performances, but surely nothing catapulted the Georgia musician to legendary status as much as his ability to add the magic ingredient of sex to the emerging rock'n'roll sound of the late-'50s. Not only did Little Richard's half-crazed singing suggest a man on the verge of orgasm himself, but his lyrics actually dared to talk about intercourse without recourse to double entendres – unheard of at the time! His first major hit, 'Tutti Frutti', was apparently the result of reworking a dirty ditty Richard was fooling around with in a recording session. Then 'Good Golly Miss Molly' just got straight down to brass tacks from the get-go.

## BEST LINES
"Good golly Miss Molly, sure like to ball/Good golly Miss Molly, sure like to ball/When you're rockin' and a rollin' can't hear your mama call."

## CAREER CONSEQUENCES
Little Richard never eclipsed those early successes. The fact that he kept ducking out of music to follow religion (and actually went to Bible college in Alabama in 1957) may have interrupted his flow somewhat. It's highly unlikely that they would have liked to ball in there.

# LL COOL J

## 'Big Ole Butt'
From *Walking With A Panther* (Def Jam, 1989)

## STYLE

Loose and funky rap based around a sparse sound of choppy guitar riff and bubbling bass, designed to highlight an everyday tale of the impossibility of fidelity with all those big bottoms out there.

## THE SORDID DETAILS

James Smith became one of the first genuine rap superstars in the mid-'80s with his first two albums, *Radio* and *Bigger And Deffer*, quickly establishing the youngster as a prime rapping force. His third release, *Walking With A Panther* was lambasted as a commercial sellout by many of his fans, but 'Big Ole Butt' still stands out as a stupidly enjoyable ode to those who are broad in the beam. "Lisa's got a big ole butt, I know I said that I'd be true/But Lisa's got a big ole butt, so I'm leaving you," says Cool James with admirable candour. And despite his stated lack of interest in fidelity, the ladies did indeed continue to love Mr Smith.

## BEST LINES

"When she walked out the door, I threw my tongue down her throat/Pushed her back inside and pulled off her coat/Laid her on the table and placed my order/And gave her a tip much bigger than a quarter/On and on to the break a dawn/All over the restaurant, word is born."

## CAREER CONSEQUENCES

Now a rap legend, LL Cool J may be one of the movement's elder statesmen and his style may sound dated, but his staying power is respected by all.

# LORDS OF ACID

## 'I Must Increase My Bust'
From *Lust* (Antler Subway, 1991)

## STYLE

Mad for it, bangin' acid house with lots of sexy talk for those who possibly might be feeling loved up.

## THE SORDID DETAILS

This Belgian-based act decided that if everybody in the acid house movement was trying to have sex (and often succeeding with the help of a little pill), then they might as well be singing about it. And sing about it is exactly what vocalist Lady Galore did on this first album. Every song was about shagging, most of the songs were about shagging while on drugs, and one of them was about shagging very roughly while on drugs. Parties round their place must have really been something. The one exception which proved the rule was this particular song which highlighted the lady's obsession with, well, with big tits. It's an obsession many can sympathise with.

## BEST LINES

"I got to admit I'm obsessed by tits/I had this problem since I was a kid/I used to look up to my auntie Marie/'Cos she had big tits hanging down to her knees/Her nipples were poking right out of her gown/If boobs gave you wings she'd be flying around/As I grew older I made up my mind/I'd get me the biggest ones I could find."

## CAREER CONSEQUENCES

The Lords continue to thrive. Female singers have come and gone, but the band's mucky mantra remains. Wonder if Lady Galore ever did get that boob job?

# LOVE/HATE

## 'Spit'
From *Wasted In America* (Columbia, 1992)

## X STYLE

Heavy metal with a quirky, almost psychedelic twist and a lyrical flow that suggested there was a little more going on inside the band members' heads than could be said of most LA rock dudes.

## X THE SORDID DETAILS

Love/Hate made much more of a splash in the UK than they ever did in their homeland, possibly due to the fact that the PMRC-infested States never really took too kindly to songs which started "met a little girl with no bloomers on" and went downhill from there. While that might sound the usual stuff of cock-rocking dreams, there's no doubt that vocalist Jizzy Pearl's lyrics had more pizzazz and style than most – in a low-down, casual sex in cockroach-infested apartments kind of way, of course. And the band's music was sufficiently twisted to mean that a tune with as low a moral threshold as 'Spit' (and I think you can guess what "put the spit on" is alluding to) still makes for interesting listening.

## X BEST LINES

"Get a little nervous/What can a poor boy say?/'Bout a girl that fucks a different guy each and every day/But she's cuddly wuddly wuddly/Too bad you don't dig dudes that play guitar/You got a thing for drummers/You got a thing for men with scars."

## X CAREER CONSEQUENCES

The law of diminishing returns. Each of Love/Hate's albums received less acclaim than its predecessor, but there's no doubt that debut *Blackout In The Red Room* and this second album had real musical substance.

# LUDACRIS

**'Area Codes'**
From *Word Of Mouf* (Def Jam, 2001)

## STYLE

Smooth, groove-heavy rap that sounds like it's had a great big portion of summer sun injected right into its beat.

## THE SORDID DETAILS

The Atlanta rapper bust out all over US urban radio in the summer of 2001 with this sparkling collaboration with Nate Dogg and Jazzy Pha. But it certainly wasn't this particular version you were hearing across the dial. Not when there was a good old grab-bag of dirty words, hoepless but fun puns (hoe-micide, hoe-liday anyone?), not to mention plenty of your straight ahead cuss words. The tune itself is solid gold and has set Ludacris up as one of the rap faces to watch.

## BEST LINES

"I bang cock in Bangkok, can't stop/I turn and hit the same spot day and night/I'm the driller in Manilla/The schlong in Hong Kong."

## CAREER CONSEQUENCES

Too early to tell. Clearly, given America's love of self-congratulation, shouting out all the phone area codes will be a big thing when Ludacris is out on the road. "Lemme hear ya'll in the 213!" Still, with a tune this good you might have to find it in your heart to forgive him.

# LUKE

## 'We Want Some Head'
From *Somethin' Nasty* (Koch, 2001)

## ✖ STYLE
Chant-a-long-a-rap with the necessary club party whoop 'n' holler atmosphere.

## ✖ THE SORDID DETAILS
Luke is the alter ego of Luther Campbell, entrepreneur and head of rap's notorious rude boys 2 Live Crew. Obviously looking for a break from 2 Live Crew's X-rated lyrical content Luke's first album, released in 1993, was titled *In The Nude* and featured songs such as 'We're Fuckin'' and 'Stop Lookin' At My Dick'. Realising that he possibly hadn't strayed quite far enough from known territory, Luke then issued 'Christmas At Luke's Sex Shop' before moving on to 1996's 'Uncle Luke'. And so it goes, right up to 2001's 'Somethin' Nasty' and 'We Want Some Head'. I defy you to suggest that Luther Campbell is a one trick pony.

## ✖ BEST LINES
"Hoes is my game/Dick in your Jones/Captain Dick is my name/Travellin' round the world turnin' bitches out/Won't you come here girl and put my dick in your mouth?"

## ✖ CAREER CONSEQUENCES
Well, you have to hand it to the man: Campbell is still at it as Luke and is still turning out mega-mucky albums, though now he defends his work under the notion that it's all about preserving the right to free speech. Ah, a true American entrepreneur still hard at work, it seems.

# THE MACC LADS

## 'Sweaty Betty'
### From *Beer & Sex & Chips'N'Gravy* (Hectic House, 1985)

## STYLE

Yob rock, pure and simple. Dim but deadly riffs, thumping drums, pounding bass and stupid songs about machismo and sex. Music to swill beer to.

## THE SORDID DETAILS

Led by top gobshite Muttley McLad, The Macc Lads blazed a trail of super sexist pub rock in the mid-'80s that immediately went against the grain of the flower-waving, miserabilist student antics of groups like The Smiths who were at that time dominating the British music press. Overtly sex-oriented and stupid, the band was clearly formed as a joke, but quickly upset all the right-on do-gooders of rock while attracting a crowd consisting mainly of morons who couldn't see the gag past the end of their noses. The inevitable irony bypass ensued.

## BEST LINES

"Sweaty Betty/She eats a lot of chips/Sweaty Betty/She's got massive tits/Sweaty Betty/She's got a huge vagina/Sweaty Betty/You'd fit a bus inside her."

## CAREER CONSEQUENCES

The joke lasted from '85 to '93, which wasn't a bad run considering the band's schtick consisted of seeing how many times they could trot out the old joke about shagging boilers and drinking way too much. And their records are as disgusting, disgraceful and dumbly amusing as ever they were.

# MADONNA

## 'Where Life Begins'
From *Erotica* (Maverick, 1992)

## STYLE

The usual whispering saucily stuff mixed in with a typically cheeky Ciccone pop tune.

## THE SORDID DETAILS

No compendium of sonic muckiness would be complete without Madonna Louise Veronica Ciccone. If the Sex Pistols' motto was "cash from chaos", then surely Madonna's was "cash from climaxes". Her own apex of sex-obsessed songs was reached with '92's *Erotica*, and 'Where Life Begins' in particular – a tune which has to be the best ode to what can only be described as "pussy licking" ever. Clearly a big fan of her tuppence being regularly serviced, it's hard to imagine that there would have been a paucity of takers for the job, which makes you wonder why she had to write a song of encouragement in the first place. Whatever the ins and outs of the story behind the song, though, 'Where Life Begins' is dirty, horny and at the same time funny, which is pretty much how the First Lady of Pop has been able to stay on top for so long, so to speak.

## BEST LINES

"Colonel Sanders says it best 'Finger lickin' good'/Let's put what you've learned to the test/Can you make a fire without using wood?/Are you still hungry; aren't you glad we came?/I'm glad you brought your raincoat, I think it's beginning to rain."

## CAREER CONSEQUENCES

Well nobody was unaware of Madonna's sexual content before this was released, so nobody would have been put off. And who knows? She might have gained a whole raft of new fans from the realms of readers of "specialist" titles.

# MANSUN

## 'Stripper Vicar'
From *Attack Of The Grey Lantern* (EMI, 1997)

## STYLE

Jaunty indie pop rock with a touch of the '60s about it. The upbeat music is in stark contrast to the sordid tale of a very British kind of sexual kinkiness.

## THE SORDID DETAILS

Forming in Chester in the mid-'90s is about as inauspicious a start as a classic rock band can get. But Mansun — hampered by location and a lack of rock star quality in their ranks — overcame the odds through sheer songwriting excellence to make their mark in the UK. Quirkiness played a part too, as this everyday tale of a local vicar who gets his kicks from stripping and wearing stockings and suspenders amply demonstrates. The tragic outcome (kinky vicar ends up bound, gagged and, frankly, dead) leaves the listener scratching his head about the meaning of this tacky, tabloidy tale of perversion. *Attack Of The Grey Lantern* made Number One, most likely on the back of major hit 'Wide Open Space' rather than this more wayward number.

## BEST LINES

"Dear Mavis thought I'd follow up my letter/Drop a line about the fate of our poor vicar/Very tragically his time on earth is ended/Found him gagged and bound in stockings and suspenders."

## CAREER CONSEQUENCES

The band have never re-scaled the heights of their debut, but are still hanging in there as one of the unlikeliest survivors of the Britpop scene.

# MARCY PLAYGROUND

## 'Sex And Candy'
From *Marcy Playground* (Capitol, 1997)

## STYLE
Ever heard Nirvana's *Unplugged* session? Well now you know exactly how 'Sex And Candy' sounds.

## THE SORDID DETAILS
Writer, guitarist and vocalist John Wozniak took his band's name from an experimental elementary school he attended as a child called The Marcy Open School. He also claimed this was a difficult period which served as a "foundation for a future self". That future self seems a tad melancholy and possibly even bitter, judging from the self-loathing broodiness of this music and Wozniak's inability to believe that the girl in the song could possibly be attracted to him. But the track nevertheless seethes with a latent sexuality that makes it seem laden with tension and the emotion of outlandish possibilities. Rude because of what it doesn't say, rather than what it does.

## BEST LINES
"I smell sex and candy here/Who's that lounging in my chair?/Who's that casting devious stares in my direction?/Mama, this surely is a dream/Mama, this surely is a dream."

## CAREER CONSEQUENCES
Big hit, platinum sales for the first album, followed by difficult sophomore effort and an instant fall from grace with *Shapeshifter*. If Wozniak was miserable beforehand, chances are he's going to be a whole lot worse now.

# MC LYTE

**'Shut The Eff Up (Hoe)'**
From *Eyes On This* (First Priority, 1989)

##  STYLE

Cool as you like bitch-rappin' from one of the first ladies of hip hop.

## THE SORDID DETAILS

Queens rapper MC Lyte was one of the first female pioneers in the hip hop world, where she quickly took her male counterparts to task over their frequently misogynistic lyrics. That didn't mean that she was all for sisterly love, though, as this vitriolic rant against a perceived rapping rival clearly demonstrates. Lyte resorts to any perceived weakness to diss her rival. From lame raps to drug use to slapperish behaviour to laughing at her obesity, no stone is left unturned in the search for the slag-off. A sharp tongue from a sharp lady.

## BEST LINES

"You get around like a cab, now that's too bad/ Everyone has been in you, isn't that sad?/Bodily vibrations? Don't make me laugh/WeightWatchers is waiting, here's a free pass."

## CAREER CONSEQUENCES

There's no doubt that Lyte opened doors for future strong female rappers such as Missy Elliott and Queen Latifah. Wonder what they make of her appearances in lame TV sitcoms like Moesha though? Perhaps they'll write a rap to diss her now.

# METHODS OF MAYHEM

**'Get Naked'**
From *Methods Of Mayhem* (MCA, 1999)

## X STYLE

Sometimes over-egged hip hop/rock crossover that tries desperately hard to sound modern. Nothing to do with big hair MTV rock.

## X THE SORDID DETAILS

When former Mötley Crüe member and husband of Pamela Anderson Tommy Lee was doing time for miscellaneous misdemeanours, the tattooed drummer decided that rootsy hip hop mixed with crunching guitars was the way forward. Subject matter for 'Get Naked' revolved around Lee's disgust at his already infamous "private" holiday video with Pammy making millions for unscrupulous Internet entrepreneurs after being stolen from their house. Of course said video wouldn't have been quite so valuable had it not featured the T-Bone fucking his wife every which way throughout, not to mention steering his holiday boat with his mammoth-sized schlong!

## X BEST LINES

**"Seven million dollars made from watchin' me cum/Under the sun on my vacation after hours on spectravision/Shootin my jizzy jizzum the woody has rizzy risen."**

## X CAREER CONSEQUENCES

Disastrous. Lee's musical career has never quite gotten over the fact that he has now become a celebrity ahead of being a drummer. What followed? Nothing musical, but a highly-public and long-running bust-up with Anderson, a relationship with Prince's former paramour Mayte and accusations from Anderson that Lee gave her hepatitis.

# GEORGE MICHAEL

'I Want Your Sex'
From *Faith* (CBS, 1988)

## STYLE
The usual middle of the roadish, slightly grindy funk from the slightly confused King of Smooch.

## THE SORDID DETAILS
Forming one of the cornerstones of Yog's 1988 solo debut, 'I Want Your Sex' appeared at the time to be a confirmation of Michael's hairy-chested, rampantly heterosexual Mr Loverman approach. In retrospect, the chest-beating bravado of the song's lyrical content takes on an altogether gayer attitude. Not that it would have stopped white-stilletoed dancefloor divas from Dagenham getting aroused if they'd known that Michael was gay. His appeal as far as the female sex was concerned had a lot more to do with the manner of his delivery than who he was personally delivering it to.

## BEST LINES
"Sex is natural, sex is good/Not everybody does it but everybody should/Sex is natural, sex is fun/Sex is best when it's one on one."

## CAREER CONSEQUENCES
Sex clearly appeared to be particularly fun for Gorgeous George when it was one on one in a Los Angeles municipal toilet! Michael was charged with lewd conduct in a men's public restroom by the LAPD in 1998, but rose above it to maintain his status as one of the world's top sexy singers. Once his homosexuality was confirmed, Michael seemed to revel in taunting his detractors by releasing ever more sexy videos that poke fun at his image as a sex symbol for the ladies.

# MINDLESS SELF INDULGENCE

## 'Pussy All Night'
From *Tight* (Uppity Cracker, 1999)

### STYLE
Kitchen sink rock/metal/hip hop/dance/industrial/anything-else-you-care-to-mention crossover.

### THE SORDID DETAILS
This New York act were nothing if not wide-screen in their vision. Trying to blend together elements of hip hop, punk rock and industrial music shows vast ambition; there's absolutely everything chucked into the melting pop here in search of the buzz. Does it work? Hard to say, it's so out-there. What we can measure with certainty is that the band don't mind a right good swear-up when there's one going, with vocalist Little Jimmy Urine leading from the front. And he doesn't much like Led Zeppelin either, if a song from their second album *Frankenstein Girls Will Seem Strangely Sexy* titled 'I Hate Jimmy Page' is anything to go by. Shall we forgive him?

### BEST LINES
*(Insert insane noises.)* "Pussy all night." *(Insert extra insane noises.)* "Come on get some" *(Add more insane noises, then stir.)*

### CAREER CONSEQUENCES
Opening slots for Rammstein and Insane Clown Posse have failed to turn Mindless Self Indulgence into household names – even in houses full of bugs where only metal records get heard!

# THE MOLDY PEACHES

**'Downloading Porn With Dave'**
From *The Moldy Peaches* (Sanctuary, 2001)

## STYLE

Super lo-fi blues rock played by folk who make a virtue of their crap credentials and a big deal out of their kookie sex lyrics.

## THE SORDID DETAILS

Kimya Dawson and Adam Green are not your average couple. For a start there's ten years between them. And then they do happen to appear on stage in rabbit suits and Robin Hood costumes when the mood takes them. Dawson claims that she feels comfortable in the rabbit suit, and we can only assume she also feels comfortable singing songs about fucking 70-year-old hookers and chicks with dicks. Such are the delights of the current New York scene, of which The Moldy Peaches predictably claim they are not a part. They claim to be serious. They don't sound it. But 'Downloading Porn With Dave' is definitely dirty.

## BEST LINES

"Sleepin' in a van between A & B/Suckin' dick for ecstasy/Paid a 70-year-old hooker to make out with me/Now the Get High Shack is just a memory."

## CAREER CONSEQUENCES

Well, everybody's current darlings The Strokes seem to like them, judging by the fact that they took the support slot on their UK tour in early 2002. Guaranteed never to sell a million records, but d'you reckon someone who dresses up in a bunny suit to perform is going to be in the slightest bit bothered by that?

# MONSTER MAGNET

**'Bummer'**
From *Powertrip* (A&M, 1998)

## STYLE

Unselfconsciously bombastic heavy metal with a slight whiff of psychedelia, all delivered with undeniable panache by vocalist Dave Wyndorf.

## THE SORDID DETAILS

Just your common or garden everyday tale of a leather-clad rocker refusing to accept the blame for all the stuff that's screwed up the head of a close female acquaintance – quite possibly the girlfriend. This may not sound like yer typical subject matter, but it's all in a day's hard-rocking work for the band that brought you 'Baby Gotterdammerung' and the unforgettable 'Negasonic Teenage Warhead'. Monster Magnet hail, incidentally, not from Valhalla, but New Jersey.

## BEST LINES

**"You're looking for the one who fucked your mum/It's not me."** *(As opening lines go, you'd have to agree that this is pretty unforgettable.)*

## CAREER CONSEQUENCES

All upside. *Powertrip* proved to be the band's breakthrough album, going gold in the States and allowing the Magnet to embark on a two-year tour supporting such rock monsters as Aerosmith, Metallica and Megadeth. Sadly, 2000's *God Says No* appeared to bum out big time. God had, indeed, said no to continued success. A return to disgraceful opening lines is surely recommended.

# JACKIE MOORE

## 'Let's Go Somewhere And Make Love'
From *Sex In The Seventies* (Sony, 1995)

##  STYLE

Smoothly does it disco/funk exhortation to all-night sauciness.

## THE SORDID DETAILS

This Florida-based singer scored a few minor R'n'B hits in the '70s with some fairly average material fleshed out by noted session players The Memphis Horns and The Dixie Flyers. This surprisingly straightforward request for horizontal action was tucked away on the B-side of a 1979 disco single 'This Time Baby', though whether this has anything to do with its lyrical sauciness or not is open to debate.

## BEST LINES

"Let's go somewhere and make love baby/From night until dawn."

## CAREER CONSEQUENCES

Besides the Indian Summer offered by disco there was no more success for Ms Moore.

# ALANIS MORISSETTE

## 'You Oughta Know'
From *Jagged Little Pill* (Maverick, 1995)

## ▨ STYLE

Slightly whiny indie rock from one-time teenie dance diva.

## ▨ THE SORDID DETAILS

The fact that Morissette was a child TV star turned dance pop artist makes this song all the more remarkable. Eschewing all the vestiges of her past the Canadian fell in with producer/musician Glen Ballard, dumped all the pop nonsense and came up with *Jagged Little Pill*, an excellent and *bona fide* rock release. Best of all, lead-off track 'You Oughta Know' was a nasty little number, a bitter and twisted look back at a relationship gone wrong. And talking about giving head in a public place certainly earned Morissette speedy alternative approval.

## ▨ BEST LINES

"Is she perverted like me?/Would she go down on you in a theatre?"

## ▨ CAREER CONSEQUENCES

Head-giving yields results. Morissette suddenly shot to mass market adult attention and found herself with a massive hit album on her hands and Grammy nominations galore. Not even for Linda Lovelace has sex proved so lucrative.

# MARK MORRISON

## 'Moan And Groan'
From *Return Of The Mack* (Atlantic, 1997)

## STYLE

Call and response ballad guaranteed to get the lady of your life in the mood and in the sack.

## THE SORDID DETAILS

If Mark Morrison had spent more time making records and less time getting up the noses of the British judicial system he might have become one of the all-time great R'n'B singers. His breakthrough single, 'Return Of The Mack', is still a magnificent tune, full of cock-sure braggadocio and delivered with a voice so transatlantic you'd never guess that the singer hailed from Leicester. As it is the jury's still out on whether Morrison will ever fulfil his considerable potential. 'Moan And Groan' is self-evident in its intentions and while it might sound lyrically slight, almost whimsical, compared to some of the serious rap stuff that's out there, in the hands of the teens and office girls who were buying his stuff it was still very rude. Girls instructing blokes to "wet them up and wet them down" good enough for you? Stereos up and down the land must have been turned down as mothers came upstairs with the washing.

## BEST LINES

"But you gotta wet me up and wet me down/I can do it (down oh yeah)/Then you gotta dry me up with some foreplay/Any problem I can solve it/Push it, work it, hurt it, all night, all night, all day."

## CAREER CONSEQUENCES

It was threatening a policeman with a stun gun rather than a few saucy lyrics that put the kybosh on our Mark's progress.

# MOTHER LOVE BONE

## 'Capricorn Sister'
From *Apple* (Polydor, 1990)

## STYLE

Groove-laden glam rock with more than a hint of Bolan influence on vocalist and lyricist Andrew Wood.

## THE SORDID DETAILS

The first stop on the musical map for soon-to-be Pearl Jammers Stone Gossard and Jeff Ament was a weird affair. Dominated by vocalist Wood's vision, there's little of the earthy rock that took Pearl Jam to the apex of the grunge movement on display here. What you get is heavily melodic hard rock sprinkled with some pretty out-there lyrics – which may well have made sense to Wood on drugs, but possibly not to those out there who prefer a pint. Still, on 'Capricorn Sister' Wood makes a heartfelt vow to cut down on his wanking time which, given his surname, may have been wholly inappropriate.

## BEST LINES

"Got my mama in the kitchen/She always bitchy bitchy bitchin'/So I made my proclamation/To control my masturbation, babe."

## CAREER CONSEQUENCES

Two trains going in different directions. Wood died of an overdose before Apple had even been released, while Ament and Gossard became two of the most successful and well-adjusted men in grunge.

# MY LIFE WITH THE THRILL KILL CULT

## 'Leathersex'
From *Sexplosion!* (Interscope, 1991)

## STYLE
Light and fluffy electronic pop with the traditional warbling female vocals for added "soul".

## THE SORDID DETAILS
Formed in Chicago in 1987, this daft electro pop band for some reason got lumped in with the much harder industrial scene, possibly for no other reason than that they wrote some songs about bondage and more extreme forms of sex. Whatever the reasoning, there's nothing to write home about in their self-consciously outrageous sound. 'Leathersex' is just as dumb as the rest of their repertoire, especially with the nonsensical line "bathe me in leather". If they were making music that sounded genuinely subversive you might buy into their schtick, but as it is they merely sound like cynical chancers.

## BEST LINES
"Groove on, assume the motion/Breathe the holy pain it resurrects/Bathe me in leather, bathe me in leather/Drown me in your sex."

## CAREER CONSEQUENCES
Now into their second decade, you have to give them full marks for tenacity. But who on earth is actually buying this stuff?

# MYSTIKAL

## 'Shake Ya Ass'
From *Let's Get Ready* (Jive, 2000)

## STYLE
James Brown style funk-o-rap with a sparse yet solid soul.

## THE SORDID DETAILS
Another rapper representing what has become known as The Dirty South, Mystikal is right up there alongside Nelly as one of the genre's prime forces. His rhymes are undoubtedly rude and crude and his voice is raw and bloodied, but he delivers them with such elan that it's hard not to be swayed in his favour. 'Shake Ya Ass', heavily supported by MTV in the States when it first emerged in 2000, is another ode to the big butt so beloved of hardcore rappers, and Mystikal is anything but subtle in his straightforward powerhouse lyrical rhyming. The bleeps on the video must have really been something!

## BEST LINES
"Now this ain't for no small booties/No sir cause that won't pass (show me whatcha workin with)/But if you feel you got the biggest one/Then momma come shake ya ass." (*Amazingly for this song there's no rude word in this section – I think we can forgive 'ass', can't we?*)

## CAREER CONSEQUENCES
Going well. Mystikal still isn't a household name in the UK, but that won't bother him too much as the man's a mega-star in the States.

# NASHVILLE PUSSY

## 'Piece Of Ass'
From *High As Hell* (TVT, 2000)

##  STYLE

Curious mixture of psychobilly and hard rock blended together through a cement mixer turned up to "11".

##  THE SORDID DETAILS

Georgia's Nashville Pussy put a marker down as to their dishonourable intentions with the release of their first major album in 1998. As if titling their magnum opus *Let Them Eat Pussy* might not give enough of a hint as to their sex-driven sound, then the cover of female members Ruyter Suys and Corey Parks being given what can only be described as "head" by two willing young men certainly gave the game away. 'Piece Of Ass' is taken from the sophomore effort *High As Hell*, which one reviewer described as having nothing to distinguish one song from the next. That's a bit harsh. What about the five second silence?

##  BEST LINES

"Some like it shaved, some like it bushy/Everyone wants some Nashville Pussy/Yeah."

##  CAREER CONSEQUENCES

Nashville Pussy are still going strong with an album, *Say Something Nasty*, released in the summer of 2002. They also have a lovely new backdrop proudly proclaiming 'In Lust We Trust'. Good to see they're keeping the flag flying.

# NECRO

## 'All Hotties Eat The Jizz'
From *Gory Days* (Psycho-Logical Records, 2001)

## STYLE
Proudly trumpeted in the Brooklyn rapper's biog as "hardcore hip hop at its sickest". For once this isn't an idle boast.

## THE SORDID DETAILS
Necro has been producing his own brand of hardcore hip hop since the early-'90s, dealing almost exclusively with the grimiest of subject matter. Drugs, death and ugly sex constantly appear in his doomy-sounding songs. In a musical style where crude lyrics and even cruder behaviour are almost prerequisites, the fact that no major label will touch this white rapper and his older rapping brother Ill Bill gives you some idea of what we're talking about here. Pressing plants refused to manufacture the original cover of *Gory Days*, featuring a girl sucking on a vibrator stuck down the barrel of a gun, which would tend to suggest that this isn't just a set of rude recordings we're dealing with here, but the work of a man with serious issues.

## BEST LINES
"My shit's for adults over eight years old only/I ran mad game son on Jenna Jameson/Just to name some, hookers that ate cum/My dick, I'm'a make Mother Teresa eat it/I'd like to treat Lisa Lisa sweet/Bitch, I'm'a fuck you like a piece of meat."

## CAREER CONSEQUENCES
Necro has promised there'll be no sell-out and that he'll be keeping it real for as long as it takes for him to become a star. Let's hope he's not holding his breath.

# NINE INCH NAILS

**'Fist Fuck'**
From *Fixed* (Nothing/Island, 1992)

##  STYLE
Bizarre industrial remix album featuring primarily reworkings from the *Broken* album of the same year.

##  THE SORDID DETAILS
Trent Reznor is the man responsible for bringing industrial music to the masses. Whereas previously this bleak and unrelenting music, driven by pounding drum beats and relentless noise-making, had been the preserve of music fans who rarely ventured out in daylight, Reznor suddenly proved that there could be tunes harnessed in with the power. 'Head Like A Hole' from the NIN debut *Pretty Hate Machine* set Reznor up as an unlikely pin-up for the movement and his influence has been widely seen in numerous nu-metal bands and especially the schlock horror work of Marilyn Manson (who he's also produced). With all the distortion on this Jim Thirlwell mix, the lyrics could be the most obscene ever; you'd never hear them. But for that gratuitously filthy title alone, this is worth a place in the 200.

##  BEST LINES
"NNNNghh/PPhnNNhhh/RRRgghhhgHHG." *(Etc., etc.)*

##  CAREER CONSEQUENCES
Spectacular. The power of noise has never been harnessed to greater commercial effect and Reznor is a genuine superstar – possibly to his own astonishment as much as everyone else's.

# NIRVANA

## 'Moist Vagina'
From Singles Box Set (Geffen, 1995)

## STYLE
Gloomy old grunge from the genre's most pained performer.

## THE SORDID DETAILS
The B-side of the 1993 'All Apologies' single released in '95 as part of the box set of all Nirvana's European singles from *Nevermind* and *In Utero*, this sounds like the rantings of a man not entirely at one with himself or his surroundings. Easy to say in retrospect, of course, but all the signs of Kurt Cobain's demise are there to be heard in this uneasy tune. Ramblings about vaginas and anuses, the repeated mantra of "marijuana", what sounds spookily like a death rattle at the end, here was not a happy camper. And this when *Nevermind* had already broken big and all should have been well with the world. Rude? Yes. Disturbing? Most definitely.

## BEST LINES
*(Well, you might as well have the lot.)* "She had a moist vagina/I particularly enjoy the circumference/I've been sucking the walls of her anus/Marijuana/I preferred her to any other/Marijuana."

## CAREER CONSEQUENCES
You know the consequences, don't you? He meant it, man…

# THE NOTORIOUS B.I.G.

## 'Fuck You Tonight'
From *Life After Death* (Bad Boy, 1997)

## STYLE

Ultra-smooth swing is aided and abetted by R. Kelly's typically silky delivery. Which makes the refrain 'I'm fucking you tonight' seem, should we say, a little less romantic than might be expected.

## THE SORDID DETAILS

Christopher Wallace was a big man with a big appetite for girls, money and the gangsta lifestyle. His prophetic album titles hinted at the fate that awaited him, so it's no wonder that Biggie Smalls wanted to shoehorn some serious living into what he expected would be a short life. Here was a man with great rapping skills, an ear for a tune and a way of making people believe his troubles and triumphs were all for real. If the lyrics to this particularly filthy tune are to be believed, The Notorious B.I.G. certainly knew how to enjoy himself horizontally. Not perhaps the tenderest man in the world, he nevertheless seemed to inspire great affection in the women he worked with, including Lil' Kim.

## BEST LINES

"Remember when I used to play between yo legs/You begged for me to stop because you know where it would head/Straight to yo mother's bed."

## CAREER CONSEQUENCES

We can only guess what other bedroom-oriented activities our man might have been willing to share with the world had he not been murdered in Los Angeles in 1997 at the height of the East versus West Coast rap wars that had already claimed Tupac Shakur.

# TED NUGENT

## 'Wang Dang Sweet Poontang'
From *Double Live Gonzo* (Epic, 1978)

## X STYLE

Insanely over-the-top, solo-fixated rock'n'roll in that good old '70s American stadium-wasting tradition.

## X THE SORDID DETAILS

Ted Nugent's role as the baiter of the liberal elite in America has all but eclipsed his contribution to hard rock music. Pro-hunting, pro-guns, ultra right wing, the Motor City Madman has gloried in getting up the noses of those who believe in a more "enlightened" attitude to life. "Balls," says Nugent, who believes liberalism has led to the moral decay of his great nation. Indeed, his anti-drug stance – a rarity in a business awash with narcotics – is something of a personal crusade. Abstaining from sex, however, clearly isn't something on the Nugent agenda, as 'Wang Dang Sweet Poontang' so eloquently explains. This 1978 live recording is introduced with a touching soliloquy: "This is a little love song. I'd like to dedicate it to all that Nashville pussy," says Ted, before launching into a frantic musical and to-the-point lyrical explanation of his infatuation with a young sex bomb.

## X BEST LINES

"She's so sweet when she yanks on my meat/Down on the street you know she can't be beat/What the hell."

## X CAREER CONSEQUENCES

Ted never bettered *Double Live Gonzo* for sheer out-and-out rock stupidity. Joining with various soft rockers to form Damn Yankees in the '80s severely damaged his cred with gumby rockers. However, Nugent seems more interested in hunting than rocking these days. He even publishes *Ted Nugent Adventure Outdoors*!

# NWA

## 'I'd Rather Fuck You'
From *Efil4zaggin* (Ruthless/Priority,1991)

## STYLE

Original gangsta rap from the daddies of all this cussin' that you're hearing on your hip hop records today. Rude.

## THE SORDID DETAILS

NWA could truly claim to have changed the music landscape with their *Straight Outta Compton* album in 1988. For the first time mainstream America got to hear how disaffected black American youth was dealing with a perceived sense of injustice… and that was by lashing out in all directions. Among valid political statements delivered with absolute street vitriol there were also songs which dealt with human issues, though all were bathed in swearing, slang and machismo. By the time *Efil4zaggin* was released in 1991, NWA had already begun to disintegrate, with prime mover Ice Cube having flown the coop after disagreements with Eric "Eazy E" Wright. Eazy threw himself into writing super-sexist smut (not your steady boyfriend type, this one!) but Dr Dre's immaculate production made NWA much more than just some rude talk. That said, 'I'd Rather Fuck You' is about as lyrically sordid as you can imagine.

## BEST LINES

"I'd rather fuck with you all goddamn night/Cause your pussy's good/Now I'm fucking all your friends/Cause you ran your mouth like I knew you would."

## CAREER CONSEQUENCES

Disastrous for Eazy. Clearly his tales of rampant screwing around were more than just idle bragging and Eric Wright succumbed to AIDS in 1995 aged just 31. The nature of his death only makes his "devil may care" attitude to sex seem even more headstrong and, frankly, loony.

# THE OHIO PLAYERS

## 'Skin Tight'
From *Skin Tight* (Mercury, 1974)

##  STYLE
Down and dirty funk with a down and dirty attitude and a down and dirty lyric to boot!

##  THE SORDID DETAILS
Starting out in Dayton (state of Ohio, of course) in 1959, The Ohio Players made their reputation as a competent R'n'B band throughout the '60s and scored a few hits along the way. But it wasn't until the '70s, a major deal with Mercury, and a series of sexy sleeves featuring good-looking women in various states of undress that the Players really hit their stride. 'Skin Tight', their first release for the new label and what sure sounds like a tribute to streetwalkers, is rightly regarded as a classic of solid funk grooves, a grinding masterpiece. In an era of blaxploitation movies where the vibes were always sassy and sexy, The Ohio Players had hit upon the perfect sleazy groove and made it pay handsomely.

##  BEST LINES
"You're a real fine lady/Yeah your walk's a little shady/Step on the strip on time/Cash money you're bound to find."

##  CAREER CONSEQUENCES
The '70s was a triumph for the band with hit following hit and classic following classic. But it was all downhill from there, and while the Players limped on through the '80s the general consensus was that their libidos had wilted.

# OL' DIRTY BASTARD

## 'I Want Pussy'
From *Nigga Please* (Elektra, 1999)

## STYLE

Spaced-out rap riding on a thin keyboard hook that sounds like it was recorded on another planet. Well, knowing ODB it very well could have been!

## THE SORDID DETAILS

Russell Jones had the world at his feet. A member of the ultra-successful Wu-Tang Clan and fêted as a true original in the world of rap, things could have been sweet were it not for the demon crack cocaine. The stories of Jones' lunatic life are many, from being shot in the back in what was supposedly a robbery at his home to being found by police with twenty bags of crack in his motor. But amid all this madness Ol' Dirty's recording life – which featured major highs both as a group member and solo – simply fell apart. 'I Want Pussy', from 1999's second solo excursion, stems from a happier time, when ODB could brag as much as he liked and get away with it. Now he sits in the Clinton Correctional Facility near the Canadian border wondering how he could have fucked it all up so badly. The usually life-affirming feel of ridiculous, dirty and OTT hip hop lyrics suddenly sound a little hollow here.

## BEST LINES

"I want pussy for free, I want pussy for free/You cannot have my money/I want pussy for free, look, I want pussy for free/I want pussy for free, I want pussy for free (for freeeeeeeee)."

## CAREER CONSEQUENCES

No label and no love for ODB right now. He's experienced so hard a comedown that Russell Jones himself says: "I don't know whether Ol' Dirty Bastard is even here any more."

145

# YOKO ONO PLASTIC ONO BAND

## 'Open Your Box (Hirake)'
From *Yoko Ono/Plastic Ono Band* (Rykodisc, 1970)

## STYLE
Difficult. That's all you need to know.

## THE SORDID DETAILS
Recorded for Yoko's first solo album, 'Open Your Box' has a clear double meaning, but might not have attracted any controversy (or, indeed, any interest) had it not also appeared on the B-side of John Lennon's 'Power To The People' single. Doubtless Yoko was attempting to make a serious political/social statement, though exactly what that might be isn't particularly easy to fathom. The BBC weren't going to be fooled by any of that either and promptly slapped a ban on the track. Given the sheer tediousness of the tune they were probably doing the listeners a favour.

## BEST LINES
"Open your box, Open your box/Open your trousers, Open your thighs/Open your legs, open, open, open, open, oooh."

## CAREER CONSEQUENCES
Ono never was one who looked all that bothered by exactly where her career would end up, and to this day she still does her own thing to the delight of some and the bemusement of many. But nobody's really interested in hearing a 69-year-old talking about leg-opening, are they?

# JOAN OSBOURNE

## 'Let's Get Naked'
From *Relish* (Mercury, 1995)

## STYLE
Slow and brooding blues rocker with a sleazy delivery for added dirtiness.

## THE SORDID DETAILS
Kentucky girl Joan Osbourne scored a massive hit straight out of the box on her major label debut with the sprightly 'One Of Us', a song later covered by no lesser a star than Prince. But hidden among the more poppy stuff is a grimy little blues song that laments the passing of the days of uncomplicated sex in a relationship and yearns for a return to it as a sign that things are still going somewhere. Osbourne uses some fine phrases along the way to make the point. "Rodeo hugs" is a particularly visual favourite.

## BEST LINES
"Let's just get naked, just for a laugh/Let's just get naked/It's a trip and a half, trip and a half/We've been together so long/I hope it wasn't just the drugs/What happened to the energy we had?/The morning glories and the rodeo hugs?"

## CAREER CONSEQUENCES
Dropped by Mercury, Osbourne returned on the Interscope label in 2000 with *Righteous Love*, which failed to make an impression.

# OUTKAST

## 'We Luv Deez Hoez'
From *Stankonia* (Arista, 2000)

## STYLE
Typically eclectic hip hop mish mash featuring a big, flappy keyboard riff and the frenetic tumbledown rapping style of Big Boi to maximum effect.

## THE SORDID DETAILS
This cautionary tale warning against the dangers of impregnating exactly the wrong kind of woman nestles almost unnoticed deep in the heart of the Atlanta duo's fourth album, the critically revered *Stankonia*. Outshone by the big hits 'So Fresh, So Clean' and 'Ms Jackson', a more than cursory listen to 'We Luv Deez Hoez' reveals a real gem of funky rap, where Big Boi leaves nothing to the imagination as he details a sexual encounter of his own with a local hoe, then berates an unidentified acquaintance for making the fool mistake of getting the girl pregnant.

## BEST LINES
"She tried to pull off my rubber with her pussy muscles/That was wrong/The bitch is no good like lesbians with no tongues."

## CAREER CONSEQUENCES
None whatsoever. Let's face it, what self-respecting rap album – even one as advanced, expansive and forward-looking as *Stankonia* – doesn't feature something smutty? But to dismiss their success as based on nothing more than sensationalism is to miss the point entirely. This is one class act – albeit with a dirty mouth!

# OVERKILL

'Fuck You'
From *Fuck You* (Megaforce EP, 1987)

## STYLE

Middle of the road thrash metal that hasn't aged with any grace. Mind you, what would you expect?

## THE SORDID DETAILS

The New York quartet were formed in 1984 and were quickly signed to Megaforce, the original indie home of Metallica. Any comparisons with the San Francisco giants ends there though. Overkill were always strictly second division, despite some entertaining soundbites delivered along the way by vocalist Bobby "Blitz" Ellsworth. 'Fuck You' proved to be their career highpoint, based on its shock value alone and an EP cover which scored low marks for subtlety. A single index finger graphically stuck in the air did, however, mean that the song did exactly what it said on the tin.

## BEST LINES

"Lie on yer backs an' comin' in trick/This you should know cause you're so cool/Yer number one, yer nobody's fool/Fuck you!" (*If anyone has the slightest idea what Overkill were on about it, I'd be delighted to hear from you.*)

## CAREER CONSEQUENCES

Overkill never really escaped the underground. Numerous guitarists came and went, but nothing changed their fortunes. You have to hand it to them for persistence, though, as Overkill were still releasing albums as recently as 2000.

# PANSY DIVISION

## 'Bill And Ted's Homosexual Adventure'
From *Pile Up* (1995)

## STYLE

Amateurish pop rock where the music most definitely isn't the message.

## THE SORDID DETAILS

This San Francisco outfit became unofficial leaders of what became known as "Queercore", a gay rock movement. If nothing else, then, gay rockers will always be known for their sense of humour. Of course the difficulty of crossing over into mass market appeal depends on writing about subject matter that people relate to, and with the best will in the world most rock fans will have a hard time making sense of 'Smells Like Queer Spirit' and 'Homo Christmas'. But there's no doubting that when they're on point Pansy Division can make you smile with their gay take on well-known subject matter. Hence 'Bill And Ted's Homosexual Adventure' spoofing on the cult film. It's funny, as is the sleeve of *Pile Up*, which features a bunch of writhing naked males at an orgy. But one joke – even a good one – wears thin in the end.

## BEST LINES

"They got condoms in their pockets/Plug into each other's sockets/They learned from Socrates/And other ancient Greeks/The art of homo love/And sexual techniques/They may not be too bright/But they know what they like/A love affair most triumphant/It's no bogus journey/It's a boner journey/It's time for Bill & Ted's Homosexual adventure to begin."

## CAREER CONSEQUENCES

Pansy Division are still going strong, with various members doing a bit of acting on the side. Don't expect platinum, but that's probably not the point anyway.

 **PATRA**

'Worker Man'
From *Worker Man* (Epic, 1994)

## ✖ STYLE
Curious mix of dancehall rapping mixed with a mainstream swinging keyboard riff.

## ✖ THE SORDID DETAILS
Clearly a lady who knows what she wants, the title track from the Jamaican singer's second album attempts to give as good on the sexual bragging front as her male counterparts in the dancehall scene. 'Worker Man' sees Patra telling the world that she does not want "a no worker" man. And if you think she means she's looking for someone who kisses her on the forehead every morning before going off to his nine to five, you're sadly mistaken. No, what Patra wants is a man who's a sexual athlete in the sack, rather than a two-minute wonder, someone who works at it. And our game girl isn't about to settle for anything less. She wants "a fifty-minute man" and a man who can "make mi do di Armstrong". Well, you would, wouldn't you?

## ✖ BEST LINES
"I want a real teddy bear/No matter how big I don't care (Hug me tight)/One who can love me up/And pour juice in my cup (Squeeze me tight)."

## ✖ CAREER CONSEQUENCES
We can only assume she found the right man, because Patra hasn't been heard of since. Let's hope she's in bed.

# PEACHES

## 'Fuck The Pain Away'
From *Teaches Of Peaches* (EFA, 2000)

## ✗ STYLE
Basic and bruising electronica that sounds sleazy, angry, filthy, amateurish and, yes, slightly frightening.

## ✗ THE SORDID DETAILS
Once referred to as a "vulgar Canadian temptress", Peaches (or Merrill Nisker, as her mum would prefer) operates on the edge of popular music, confusingly mixing what appears to be an aspiration toward high art with a sex-centric obsession that seems to enjoy wallowing in the gutter. In a world where sex sells, the pink leather-shirted Peaches still remains something of a secret because she looks and sounds disturbing and turns sex into something worriesome. Anyone who can open a song with the line "Sucking on my titties" (as she does in 'Fuck The Pain Away') without it sounding remotely horny has to be doing something at least, well, innovative. And that, of course, is entirely the point.

## ✗ BEST LINES
"Suckin' on my titties like you wanted me/Calling me all the time."

## ✗ CAREER CONSEQUENCES
Destined for the underground unless she finds a way to retain her own values while writing more commercially. Peaches needs to sing about sex as less of a crusade and more of a sport.

# PLASMATICS

### 'Sex Junkie'
From *Beyond The Valley Of 1984* (Stiff America, 1981)

## STYLE
An average punk/glam mish-mash held together by the sticky tape of an outrageous look and a title designed to draw attention.

## THE SORDID DETAILS
Wendy Orleans Williams originally made her name as a porno model and actress and haphazardly ended up in the music business when porn entrepreneur Rod Swenson veered into the music game. He became the manager of The Plasmatics, she became the singer and they became lovers. The band were famous for their outrageous stage sets and Williams gained notoriety for wearing almost nothing on stage and for brandishing a chainsaw. The music – whether the band liked it or not – was secondary to the shock value they provided and The Plasmatics never made anything more than a temporary splash on the scene. Yet beneath the shock and outrage, the song 'Sex Junkie' also hinted at a despair in the singer. It's less a homage to a voracious sexual appetite than you might expect and more a bitter diatribe against men who can't see further than the end of their dicks.

## BEST LINES
"Your thing it grows and grows and grows/Sex hormones dropped from out of the sky/Millions orgasm until they die/Squirming flesh you beg for more/You live for sex/There is no more/Eat me."

## CAREER CONSEQUENCES
After retiring from the spotlight as the '80s drew to a close, Williams and Swenson retired to Connecticut, but a quiet exit never seemed to be Williams' style and she committed suicide by shooting herself on April 6, 1998.

153

# THE POLICE

## 'Be My Girl – Sally'
From *Outlandos D'Amour* (A&M, 1978)

## STYLE

Spoken word silliness as a precursor to the usual white reggae lolloping and helium-inflated vocals of Gordon Sumner

## THE SORDID DETAILS

Rightly lambasted as plastic punks, The Police would soon have the last laugh with phenomenal worldwide success. But on this, their debut album, it's clear they needed to find themselves some spittle-flecked street cred from somewhere. After all, this was a band with a drummer who'd been in Curved Air and a guitarist who'd played with Neil Sedaka! The result was 'Be My Girl – Sally', a pretty stupid, mainly spoken-word piece about the pleasures of having it off with one of those plastic dolls ("with realistic hair") that can still be found in the back pages of certain "specialist" magazines. Hey, now that was really punk! Doubtless rain forest campaigner and general all-round gent Sting won't be putting this on his Tracks I'm Proud To Have Been Part Of car tape.

## BEST LINES

"I took her to the bedroom and pumped her with some life/And later in a moment that girl became my wife/And so I sit her in the corner and sometimes stroke her hair/And when I'm feeling naughty I blow her up with air."

## CAREER CONSEQUENCES

Crap songs about crap activities didn't stop 'Roxanne', 'So Lonely' and 'Can't Stand Losing You' from setting The Police on their way to superstardom.

# POP WILL EAT ITSELF

## 'Beaver Patrol'
From *Box Frenzy* (Chapter 22, 1987)

## STYLE
Enthusiastic if unrefined attempt to meld together rugged guitar rock with nascent hip hop tendencies via an obscure '60s cover version.

## THE SORDID DETAILS
Pop Will Eat Itself managed to make an art form out of stupidity. Emerging as a backlash against the ever more po-faced British indie scene, the Poppies originally performed fast tempo, guitar-driven pop, but quickly assimilated limited rap influences in time for their debut album, *Box Frenzy*, to be making tentative steps toward the 'sampling and lager' sound which soon became their signature. 'Beaver Patrol' sits somewhere between the two styles with a deliberately dumb lyric made even dumber by it being so inappropriate for an English band.

## BEST LINES
"I pull in the drive, I shut off the key/I say to the girl, 'Will you sit by me?'/I say to her 'Darlin' what's your name?'/I say to myself, 'I'm proud I came'."

## CAREER CONSEQUENCES
Mission accomplished. Idiocy, sexism and memorability all rolled into one. The very notion that these lads would "Get their kicks" from "hustling chicks" in a beaver patrol on the mean streets of Stourbridge was laughable. But the band were very much in on the joke and continued to make a half-decent career out of the very same values for quite some time.

# THE PRESIDENTS
# OF THE UNITED
# STATES OF AMERICA

### 'Stranger'
From *Presidents Of The United States Of America*
(Columbia, 1995)

##  STYLE

Slightly kooky indie rock from a band who took grunge and tried to
make it fun.

## THE SORDID DETAILS

While most Seattle acts of the early-'90s were busy getting depressed
and taking drugs, The Presidents Of The United States Of America
managed to play the music without getting the blues. Vocalist Chris
Ballew seemed too damned happy to be part of the scene and indeed
The Presidents were never taken to the hearts of the Flannel-Shirt
Wearers Association. That didn't stop them having a massive hit debut
album, though, and a couple of big singles in 'Lump' and 'Peaches'.
This quiet/loud/quiet/loud affair mentions someone in a Lynyrd Skynyrd
hat, which in itself is genius, but then referring to a girl who seems cool
"for a naked chick in a booth" obviously gets double points.

## BEST LINES

"Carla the stripper, straight from LA/You seem cool for a naked
chick in a booth/Let's be pals someday (in other words)/Put some
clothes on and call me."

## CAREER CONSEQUENCES

The Presidents never seemed that arsed about what was happening to
them and after what they doubtless considered a good run ("thanks for
our houses!") they called it quits in 1998.

# PRINCE

### 'Jack U Off'
From *Controversy* (Warner Bros, 1981)

## STYLE

Ridiculously poppy R'n'B which quickly lulls you into a false sense of security. And then Prince starts singing...

## THE SORDID DETAILS

Prince's fourth album picked up just where *Dirty Mind* had finished off a year earlier, with the stocking-wearing Minneapolis boy finding it tough to write about anything other than what was between his legs. 'Jack U Off', the last number on a super-short album (eight tracks, just about thirty-five minutes), shows off Prince's more, well, "sensitive" side. Here he kindly puts his partner's climactic pleasure before his own, explaining the many and varied locations in which he intends to bring the object of his affections to the point of climax. These include a movie theatre, restaurant, car and, disappointingly conventional, "the sack".

## BEST LINES

"If you really really wanna be a star/You gotta do it in your mama's car/Naked in a Cadillac/I'll jack u off."

## CAREER CONSEQUENCES

Prince won over the critics with such displays of lasciviousness and barefaced cheek, then sucker-punched the general public with his next album, the double 1999. Refining his muckiness into something a little more friendly, tunes like 'Little Red Corvette' and the title track sent Prince's career into orbit. In over twenty years, though, the joy of sex has never been too far from the wee one's mind.

PRINCESS SUPERSTAR

'Bad Babysitter'
From *Princess Superstar Is* (!K7/Rapster, 2002)

##  STYLE

Fun and fresh slow-grooving hip hop with a wicked girl fronting up the sauce.

## THE SORDID DETAILS

Lazily called the female Eminem because she's white and talks dirty, this native New Yorker is no bandwagon jumper with a filthy mouth. Though she does love the rude stuff. At it since 1996's debut *Strictly Platinum* (it wasn't) and combining that mucky tongue with a giant-sized sense of humour, Concetta Kirschner suddenly broke through into the mainstream in 2002 with 'Bad Babysitter', a fun tale of earning six bucks an hour looking after someone else's kids while making sure that she gets some more adult fun of her own into the bargain. Silly, smutty and guaranteed to put a smile on your face.

## BEST LINES

"All right kid u gotta go 2 bed/I know its only six but my boy just came over and he wants me 2 give him head/Sit his bare ass where u watch Small Wonder/Next time u watch Vicky the spot'll be sticky coz I sucked his dicky and used your mom's cucumber/Don't worry I'll put it back."

## CAREER CONSEQUENCES

It's early days as yet for the eight year overnight success, so it's hard to tell whether this particular blonde will be able to match the success of Eminem. Of course she will object to being compared to him here. And as she once rapped "Everyone calls me the female Eminem/Well all I'm gonna talk about is getting fucked up the arse". Smashing!

# PULP

**'Pencil Skirt'**
From *Different Class* (Island, 1995)

## STYLE
Curtain-twitching sex and suburbia theme supported by a claustrophobic atmosphere of brooding indie pop.

## THE SORDID DETAILS
Jarvis Cocker adopts the character of a suburban lothario who nips round a local lass' gaff to instruct her in what is commonly called "The Ways Of Love". This kind of grimy suburban morality play (minus the morals) made Pulp a Britpop phenomenon in the mid-'90s, and who better to play out the roles than the increasingly louche Cocker, a geeky misfit who eventually turned public opinion through 360 degrees and became cool and fashionable? Not one of the best moments from their breakthrough album, as it happens, especially when it's followed by the sensational 'Common People'. But for sheer scuzz it takes some beating.

## BEST LINES
"When you raise your pencil skirt like a veil before my eyes/Like the look upon his face as he's zipping up his flies/Oh I know that you're engaged to him/Oh but I know you want something to play with baby."

## CAREER CONSEQUENCES
*Different Class* put Pulp into the bracket of bona fide pop superstars for a couple of years, especially when Cocker attempted to upstage Michael Jackson by invading his stage at the Brit awards. But nothing the band have produced since has matched their magnum opus.

# SHABBA RANKS

### 'Wicked Inna Bed'
From *Rough & Ready Vol. 1* (Epic, 1992)

## ✕ STYLE

The earliest working example of reggae rap, the combination of
Jamaican dancehall and American hip hop pioneered by this many times
self-proclaimed sexual athlete.

## ✕ THE SORDID DETAILS

Rexton Rawlston Fernando Gordon always had an eye on making his
name as a DJ and performer, starting out at the age of 14 in Kingston
and making his way by the mid-'80s to the position of most in-demand
DJ in the whole of the West Indies. As you might guess, this reputation
wasn't made on the back of church-going, consciousness-raising
material. Shabba made a big thing of gangster violence and a big thing
of his, well, big thing. 'Wicked Inna Bed' is a pretty straightforward
message delivered straightforwardly. There is no room to doubt that
Shabba's wicked in bed given that he tells us approximately 134 times
during the course of the track. Woe betide him if any lady he bedded
left feeling unsatisfied. His reputation would have been in tatters.

## ✕ BEST LINES

"Wicked inna bed and mad inna bed, wicked in a bed I'm mad and
wicked/And all the girls tell the world/I'm a wicked inna bed and
mad inna bed."

## ✕ CAREER CONSEQUENCES

Shabba moved seamlessly into the mainstream and had success in the
'90s with tracks like 'Mr Loverman' and 'Slow And Sexy'.
Unsurprisingly, this additional success didn't make him any less cocky
about his tackle's potential.

# RED HOT CHILI PEPPERS

## 'Suck My Kiss'
From *BloodSugarSexMagic* (Warner Bros, 1991)

## ✖ STYLE

Fits into the much dreaded and harangued term of funk metal, but without the connotations it describes the sound admirably.

## ✖ THE SORDID DETAILS

Do you reckon the guide lyrics for this track really went "Suck my kiss"? Really think so? Have you checked those lyrics really closely? On the sleeve of BloodSugarSexMagic it claims that the second chorus of 'Suck My Kiss' is just a repeat of the first. Listen closely and you'll find that's not true. And therein lies the secret of what this song is really all about. Aha. Mind you, you could probably have worked it out for yourself just by thinking about it for a second. And this is Anthony Kiedis we're talking about, a man so preoccupied with his penis that he's often performed with nothing but a sock covering it. They do stuff like that in LA.

## ✖ BEST LINES

"Hit me you can't hurt me/Suck my kiss/Kiss me please, pervert me/Stick with this/Is she gonna curtsy/Give to me sweet sacred bliss/That mouth was made to suck my kiss."

## ✖ CAREER CONSEQUENCES

The Chilis have had problems with drugs (like, band members dying kinda problems), but every setback seems to make them stronger and the band's last album, *Californication*, was their biggest yet.

# BUSTA RHYMES

## 'Give It To Me Raw'
From *Extinction Level Event* (Elektra/Asylum, 1998)

## STYLE

Built around a repeated riff of Chinese music (no kidding!) and delivered slow tempo to make you, like, listen to the words.

## THE SORDID DETAILS

One of the rap scene's most outrageous, intelligent and original artists, Busta Rhymes has made his name thanks to a style of delivery that owes as much to ragga as traditional hip hop. Born in Brooklyn to Jamaican parents and raised on Long Island, Busta's hip hop education began as a 17-year-old member of Leaders Of The New School, who'd recorded two acclaimed albums by 1993. Out on his own Busta soon claimed his own turf with a wild style mixed with expansive and eclectic musical backdrops. A true original: even when giving just as rude a rhyme as any of his rivals, Rhymes twists the lyric to deliver a cautionary tale of girls who are prepared to drop their panties just to get a hold of your cash stack.

## BEST LINES

"Pussy made me feel like I was drugged up on morphine/My movie screen ass stacking more than we've all seen/Yo, chick 'bout to make me wile on her real hard/A real fraud, fuck I ever fucked with this ill broad/Chick still after my loot, she like: 'What, son?'/Don't act dumb scheming on a robbery outcome."

## CAREER CONSEQUENCES

It's tunes like this that made Busta Rhymes. Kooky, off-beat, interesting and yet still accessible, no wonder he's one of rap's biggest stars.

# ROCK BITCH

## 'Essex Girl'
From *Motor Driven Bimbo* (Steamhammer, 1999)

## STYLE
Metal played by women who sound like men but look like women but act like men. Have you got the picture now?

## THE SORDID DETAILS
Doubtless Rock Bitch would be suitably offended to be referred to as in any way sordid, though most people might find their creed a little hard to stomach. The band's website says it best. "Rock Bitch are a group of female musicians who come from a sex commune. The community consists of many more persons than are in the band, but has only three male members. All the women are lesbian or bisexual, there are no exclusive monogamous couples. The community has been based in France for ten years, it was the dream of Amanda (The Bitch, The Bass) to create a feminist, matriarchal, tribal retreat where women could explore their sexuality and psyche." So all that cool stuff that may have titillated you – the live-on-stage sex, the platinum condom that wins a lucky audience member the chance to have it off with one or more band members – is actually a political statement. Beats New Labour, though.

## BEST LINES
"No sex please we're British? You must be fucking joking!/The British are the kinkiest people on the planet/I've fucked every nationality – and I'm tellin' ya/There's no-one dirtier than an...Essex girl!"

## CAREER CONSEQUENCES
Well there's been no album since 1999, but www.rockbitch.co.uk is very much an active website, full of explanations of the ethos behind the band, tour dates and plenty of very rude pictures indeed.

# THE ROLLING STONES

## 'Cocksucker Blues'
From *Cocksucker Blues* (blank bootleg, 1977)

## STYLE
Mournful acoustic blues lament, focusing on Jagger's typically southern-inflected vocal delivery of a gay hooker's trials and tribulations.

## THE SORDID DETAILS
'Cocksucker Blues', so legend has it, was written by Mick Jagger as a contractual fulfilment song when the band were signed to Decca. When Jagger played the demo of the tune – a graphic account of a gay prostitute working the streets of London – to the stuffy Decca execs the desired effect was achieved and the song was never released. This seedy episode then provided the inspiration for the title of a movie of The Stones' legendarily debauched North American tour of 1972, a 90-minute montage of predominantly sex and drugs, with the occasional bit of rock'n'roll thrown in, possibly for contractual fulfilment.

## BEST LINES
"Oh where can I get my cock sucked?/Where can I get my ass fucked?/I may have no money/But I know where to put it every time."

## CAREER CONSEQUENCES
Once the Stones got to view the finished version of Robert Frank's film, they decided it wasn't really the kind of thing they wanted their mums to see and got a court injunction against its distribution. Otherwise, they've muddled through ever since.

# MAX ROMEO

## 'Pussy Watchman'
From *Wet Dreams* (Esoldun, 1993)

## STYLE
Simplistic reggae with a lecherous and testosterone-heavy lyrical touch.

## THE SORDID DETAILS
Hailing from Kingston, Maxwell Smith gained his nickname from a tale of having been spotted chatting up a girl one morning, only to have been seen in exactly the same spot still chatting up the same girl eight hours later. Romeo first became known when his song 'Wet Dream' was banned by the BBC in the late-'60s on the grounds that it was too suggestive. Romeo raised a spirited but preposterous defence that the song was in actual fact about a leaky roof, but even the BBC's old guard weren't about to fall for that one, not when he was also recording songs with titles such as 'My Dickie' (about a formal tie, perhaps?) and 'Pussy Watchman'. Of course the ban only served to make more people interested in the record and 'Wet Dream' stormed into the Top 10.

## BEST LINES
"You are a pussy watchman, that's why you have one eye/You are a fanny watchman, that's why you have one eye."

## CAREER CONSEQUENCES
In the '70s Max Romeo underwent a radical spiritual transformation and renounced his libidinous former self. Becoming a Rastafarian, Romeo set about writing more cerebral material and even worked with production guru Lee "Scratch" Perry on his new songs of higher calling.

# TODD RUNDGREN

'Slut'
From *Something/Anything?* (Bearsville, 1972)

## STYLE
Self-deprecating boogaloo that gives meatheads something to swill beer to, while the songwriter looks on in wry amusement.

## THE SORDID DETAILS
The very last of twenty-five tracks featured on one of Rundgren's most revered releases, the story is a simple one: Rundgren – geeky of posture and long of hair – is checking out a girl on the dance floor and nodding in approval. His infatuation with the object of his affections doesn't stop him being able to take a certain detached view, commenting on the sagginess of her thighs. However, despite his acceptance that the object of his affections may indeed be a little on the loose side, she nevertheless retains all of her sexual appeal. Which is nice. The band barks out a helpful spelled out refrain to leave us in no doubt as to what they think of the girl.

## BEST LINES
"S-L-U-T/She may be a slut, but she looks good to me."

## CAREER CONSEQUENCES
Nobody was going to be bothered about rogue musical trader Todd Rundgren writing an offensive little song like this. Rundgren has been positively lauded for his lack of respect for traditional conventions. A dirty little ditty recorded for fun – and taken as such.

# SALT 'N' PEPA

## 'Let's Talk About Sex'
From *Blacks' Magic* (Polygram, 1990)

## STYLE

Commercial hip hop with a brazen and unapologetically poppy feel from the New York all-girl trio.

## THE SORDID DETAILS

The very fact that Salt 'n' Pepa were out there at all as an all-female rap act (including female DJ Spinderella even!) in a male-dominated world speaks volumes for them. The fact that these sisters could do it for themselves while still retaining a real femininity and sexiness is all the more praiseworthy. 'Let's Talk About Sex' certainly stirred the pants of millions of young men all over the world and the three Brooklyn girls' relaxed attitude to the old in-out-in-out felt particularly naughty and subversive in the post-AIDS world. No doubt Salt 'n' Pepa's commercial feel helped spread the message that there's nothing wrong with sex far further afield than the traditional hip hop community. Suburbia would never be the same again. And nor would teenage boys' bedsheets.

## BEST LINES

"Ladies, all the ladies, louder now, help me out/Come on, all the ladies – let's talk about sex! All right/Yo, Pep, I don't think they're gonna play this on the radio/And why not? Everybody has sex/I mean, everybody should be makin' love/Come on, how many guys can fuck like my man?"

## CAREER CONSEQUENCES

Our girls have been pretty quiet since the mid-90s, trying their hand at acting and even opening a chain of clothing stores.

# SCORPIONS

## 'Don't Make No Promises (Your Body Can't Keep)'
from *Animal Magnetism* (Harvest, 1980)

## STYLE
Not so heavy heavy-metal from the open-mouthed (and now balding) German stompers

## THE SORDID DETAILS
The Scorpions became a major rock attraction in the mid-'80s by toning down their earlier Hendrix obsessions and ceasing to put almost-artistic shots of women's breasts on their album sleeves. The metamorphosis began with 1980's *Animal Magnetism*, but the band were still obsessed with the potential deviance in sexual encounters that they'd first explored in the hilariously naïve-sounding 'He's A Woman, She's A Man' (yes, it was about a transsexual). Here vocalist Klaus Meine investigates the illusory nature of the rock groupie who turns out to be not quite what she seems when the horny singer gets her back to his hotel for action. Rude and stupid at one and the same time.

## BEST LINES
"Next day, can you believe, she was at the show/She said, 'Hey man, you're great,' and she took me home/She started to undress, what a shock to see/Padded bra, blonde wig, not much left for me."

## CAREER CONSEQUENCES
Nobody held these sixth-form sexual scribblings against the band, presumably charitably realising that they were, after all, writing in a foreign language, bless 'em.

# SEX PISTOLS

## 'Friggin' In The Riggin''
From *The Great Rock'n'Roll Swindle* (Virgin, 1979)

 **STYLE**

Rousing pub rock performed (it is hoped) while the band was drunk. It's certainly the best way to listen to it.

**THE SORDID DETAILS**

As The Sex Pistols began to implode under the pressures of being a bunch of young idiots with money for the first time, 'Friggin' In The Riggin'' emerged as part of the *The Great Rock'n'Roll Swindle* double. At the time of its release this soundtrack to what was a documentary of sorts was seen as the cheapest, tackiest sell-out and a personal affront to the many who had embraced the whole punk ethos. And granted, the idea of putting what was effectively a bawdy rugby song to a joke punk backing can't be seen as high art. But let's not forget that Steve Jones had by now taken to wearing a knotted hanky on his head, so what did anyone expect?!

## BEST LINES

"The second mate was Andy/By Christ he was a dandy/Till they crushed his cock on a jagged rock/For cuming in the brandy."

**CAREER CONSEQUENCES**

Less than eighteen months after the explosive release of *Never Mind The Bollocks...*, the Sex Pistols found themselves turning into some kind of bizarre blue cabaret act. Johnny Rotten had long since left in disgust and the whole affair had turned into a "Get Rich Quick" scheme for those less scrupulous. Ironically, 'Friggin' In The Riggin'' was released as a single B-side to the old rock'n'roll standard 'Something Else' in the same month, February of '79, that Sid Vicious died of a drugs overdose. Ever had the feeling you've been cheated?

# SHAKIRA

## 'Underneath Your Clothes'
From *Laundry Service* (Sony, 2001)

## X STYLE

Jaunty pop with slight Latino flavour from the Colombian saucepot who either doesn't quite know what she's singing about – or is even more raunchy than she appears!

## X THE SORDID DETAILS

Shakira introduced herself to mainstream Western pop culture with a song about the size of her breasts. Or more accurately her own appraisal of them in her breakout hit 'Whenever, Wherever'. "Lucky that my breasts are small and humble/So you don't confuse them with mountains," says the 25-year-old. Lucky, indeed, though if anyone actually did confuse boobs with mountains they would surely be a suitable case for psychiatric help. No matter, Shakira's got more where that came from, as evidenced by this cheeky little number. Is this the kind of filth that our pop kids should be subjected to? Maybe they just do things a little different down Colombia way.

## X BEST LINES

**"Don't get me wrong 'cos this might sound to you a bit odd/But you own the place where all my thoughts go hiding/And right under your clothes is where I find them."**

## X CAREER CONSEQUENCES

All systems go for the attempt at world domination. Lack of English language skills in the lyrical department hasn't harmed Shakira's prospects one jot.

170

# SIR MIX-A-LOT

## 'Baby Got Back'
From *Mack Daddy* (Def America, 1991)

## STYLE
Two tons of fun rap and roll from a man who likes big butts and who cannot lie!

## THE SORDID DETAILS
The very idea that anyone could have got out of their prams for a black man celebrating big butts is laughable. But that's what happened when Seattle's Sir Mix-A-Lot released his tongue-in-cheek single that turned into a monster hit. Far from praising Caesar for coming out and saying that he literally couldn't be arsed with skinny girls from rock videos and preferred a bit of meat on the bone, Mix-A-Lot was lambasted for sexism toward skinny girls. It seems that there was a worldwide sense of humour failure in 1991. Had the offended parties known what kind of lyrics were just around the corner in the world of rap, do you think they would have kicked up such a stink?

## BEST LINES
"So I'm lookin' at rock videos/Knockin' these bimbos walkin' like hoes/You can have them bimbos/I'll keep my women like Flo-Jo/A word to the thick soul sistas/I wanna get with ya/I won't cuss or hit ya/But I gotta be straight when I say I wanna uurgh/Til the break of dawn/Baby got it goin on."

## CAREER CONSEQUENCES
Those pesky meddlin' feminists must have gotten their way. Sir-Mix-A-Lot never quite made as much chart noise again. Curse you do-gooders!

# SLEEPER

**'Swallow'**
From *Smart* (Indolent, 1995)

##  STYLE

Energetic and enthusiastic if naïve-sounding Britpop delivered by the undoubtedly rude and sexy Louise Wener.

## THE SORDID DETAILS

Sleeper caused a minor furore in the UK with their debut album *Smart*, mainly because of the catchy hit single 'Inbetweener' and the fact that frontwoman Wener seemed happy to acknowledge her sexual feelings and desires on disc and then discuss them with the press. One lyric which caused some excitement among 20-something male music writers was: "We should both go to bed till we make each other sore," but 'Swallow' was ruder still, charting the kind of dysfunctional relationship where sex is all about pain rather than pleasure.

## BEST LINES

"There he comes/She swallows." *(Subtle it was not.)*

## CAREER CONSEQUENCES

Mucky lyrics alone couldn't save Sleeper and as the infatuation with Britpop started to wane Sleeper found themselves out in the cold and split in 1998. Wener has since turned her hand to writing chick-lit novels and had *Goodnight Steve McQueen* published in 2002.

# SLICK RICK

## 'Treat Her Like A Prostitute'
From *The Great Adventures Of Slick Rick* (Def Jam, 1988)

##  STYLE

Proto gangsta rapping from Wimbledon-born Ricky Walters whose family emigrated to the Bronx in the late-'70s.

## THE SORDID DETAILS

Slick Rick may not be the biggest name in hip hop's pantheon, but his flash style, trademark eyepatch (not just an affectation, but the result of being blinded by broken glass as a child) and misogynistic lyrics provided a blueprint for much of what was to follow. Had a prison sentence not intervened (for shooting at a cousin and then leading the cops on a wild car chase), who knows what might have happened? But *The Great Adventures Of Slick Rick* is still a benchmark work in self-aggrandising sex talk and put-downs of no-good hoes. Which is a recommendation of sorts.

## BEST LINES

"Next thing you know, the ho starts to ill/She says, 'I love you, Harold' and your name is Will/That's not the half 'til you start to ride her/Take off your rubber and there's one more inside her/It's not yours – who can it be?/I think it was a slick rapper, his name is M.C. Ricky."

## CAREER CONSEQUENCES

Prison trouble aside, The Slick One came back with 1999's *The Art Of Storytelling*, which was greeted with indifference.

**SMEARS**

'Cum Into My Mouth'
From *Smears In The Garage* (Dionysus, 1995)

## STYLE

Trashy, amateurishly-produced, poorly-played garage pop. Apart from that, excellent.

## THE SORDID DETAILS

These ladies from Bloomington, Indiana (home of John Mellencamp) did not want to be messed with. Sporting a bass with a sticker saying "Suck Cock", Gretchen Holz was a brassy lady taking on the guys at their own game. Smears specialised in songs that pointed out the pain that goes with sexual relationships with men, who all appear to be self-centred assholes and who are only really worth sneering at and possibly shagging for personal gratification. Why not? It's what plenty of blokes have been thinking for years.

## BEST LINES

"I want to taste that cum on my tongue/Cum into my mouth."

## CAREER CONSEQUENCES

Ignored at every turn, Smears are the living proof that a few rude records do not a career make.

# BESSIE SMITH

### 'Empty Bed Blues'
From *Incomparable* (Columbia River, 1999)

## STYLE
Beautifully delivered saucy blues from one of the style's greatest singers.

## THE SORDID DETAILS
Known as "The Empress Of The Blues", Bessie Smith was the first major blues stylist recorded way back in 1923. Her astonishingly soulful voice still manages to cut through the low quality of those early recordings and she was the major face of the movement throughout the '20s. Her summer shows, provocatively titled "Harlem Frolics", were a massive hit between 1925 and 1927. Bessie's lust for life and love meant she was perfectly prepared to sing words that would have been (rightly) seen as close to the knuckle and she made no apologies for it.

## BEST LINES
"He poured my fat cabbage and made it awful hot/When he put in his bacon it overflowed the pot/Lord he's got that sweet something and I told my girlfriend Lou/From the way she's raving she must and gone and tried it too."

## CAREER CONSEQUENCES
Sadly, Bessie's career dived in the '30s as the blues went out of fashion. Dropped by Columbia in 1931 she kept working right the way up until her untimely death in 1937 in a car crash in Mississippi. She was aged just 43.

# SOFT CELL

## 'Sex Dwarf'
From *Non Stop Erotic Cabaret* (Sire, 1981)

## STYLE
Super sleazy synthetic synth pop that expertly creates an atmosphere of rubber-hooded malevolence. Notable for using the distorted vocal so beloved of 21st-century goth acts such as Marilyn Manson and Nine Inch Nails more than twenty years later.

## THE SORDID DETAILS
Track five on this dirty 1981 release perfectly summed up the heavy, S&M-ish attitude of the first Soft Cell album, *Non Stop Erotic Cabaret*. With camp frontman Marc Almond revelling in his deviance, Dave Ball's pounding synth lines were made for the dank, dark and degenerate strip clubs of London's Soho. 'Sex Dwarf' sounds as hopelessly subsumed by filth as the day it was released.

## BEST LINES
"I would like you on a long black leash/I would parade you down the high street/ You've got the attraction, you've got the pulling power/Walk my little doggy, walk my little sex dwarf."

## CAREER CONSEQUENCES
It seemed as if the public never got over the oppressive seediness of the duo's debut album. 'Sex Dwarf' itself never garnered mass attention, dwarfed as it was by the massive hit 'Tainted Love'. Soft Cell continued to plough their own peculiar dirtbag furrow, but by the time 1984's *This Last Night In Sodom* was released, most of the paying public had simply opted to sod 'em altogether and a break-up was inevitable. Music that was and still is strictly for the underground.

# SOUNDGARDEN

### 'Big Dumb Sex'
From *Louder Than Love* (A&M, 1989)

## STYLE
Raucous, screaming heavy-metal disguised as grunge from the most traditional of the Seattle wave of the early '90s. Only distinguishable from the real deal because of its tongue-in-cheek approach to lyrical content.

## THE SORDID DETAILS
One of the first groups to be signed to the legendary Sub Pop label, Soundgarden's love for the sound but distaste for the attitudes of traditional rock bands led to lyrics such as 'Big Dumb Sex', a clearly ironic stab at writing a shagging song, which of course ended up being much ruder than the songs it was attempting to pastiche. Chris Cornell's primal scream as he tenderly explains that he's really, definitely, absolutely going to fuck the object of his desires is quite one of the most frightening scenarios ever played out in the world of music!

## BEST LINES
"Hey I know what to do/I'm gonna fuck, fuck, fuck, fuck you/Fuck you."

## CAREER CONSEQUENCES
Not much radio play for this one, rather predictably, but through dogged persistence Soundgarden eventually matched their brighter-burning Seattle peers such as Nirvana and Alice In Chains, scoring major hits with 'Fell On Black Days' and 'Black Hole Sun' from 1994's *Superunknown* before splitting in 1997.

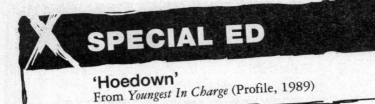

# SPECIAL ED

'Hoedown'
From *Youngest In Charge* (Profile, 1989)

##  STYLE

Gimmicky hip hop mixing a decent mic style with a hickey banjo riff groove. 'Hoedown.' Geddit?

## THE SORDID DETAILS

Brooklyn's Special Ed burst on to the scene in 1989 with *Youngest In Charge*, a precocious album from the 16-year-old rapper. Featuring the usual bragging and boasting, it could have been easy for such a young MC to fall flat on his arse. But Ed's skills on the mic meant that he could hold his own with the bigger boys. Sadly, 'Hoedown' is one of the dumbest tracks on the debut, where the young buck is trying to convince us all that he's having as much and better sex as any one of his rapping contemporaries. It's gimmicky – lyrically and musically – and no doubt LL Cool J would have had something to say about who was really having the most and best sex back in '89.

## BEST LINES

"Put her hands on my pants, the zipper was zippin'/Laid me down on the couch, sat down on my hip, and straddled up, and then she took a dip/And the girl was sweeter than a chocolate chip/And I called her name out loud, I said, 'Jodie – oh!'/I said, 'You must be down with the rodeo the way you ride/It might sound silly but you're ridin up and down like Bronco Billy'."

## CAREER CONSEQUENCES

Special Ed proved to be not that special after all, at least in terms of sales. His third album, *Revelations* appeared in 1995, but still contained the same amount of bragging. The schtick had worn thin and Ed disappeared.

# SPINAL TAP

## 'Big Bottom'
From *Music From The Original Motion Picture Soundtrack* (Polydor, 1984)

## STYLE
Bum-thumping heavy metal from the scene's undoubted maestros.

## THE SORDID DETAILS
Spinal Tap has blurred the edges of fantasy and reality in music better than any other spoof project and nearly twenty years after its original release it is still quoted almost daily by music industry folk. The secret of its success lies not only in the accuracy of its portrayal of rock peccadilloes (not to be confused with armadillos – down the trousers), but also in the fact that the actors were musicians who could write great awful metal tunes to order. Biggest and best of all is 'Big Bottom', an ode to the fuller rump that precedes the classic rap anthem, Sir Mix-A-Lot's 'Baby Got Back' by fully eight years! Now that takes skill, the St Hubbins/Tufnell writing partnership in full effect.

## BEST LINES
"The bigger the cushion/The sweeter the pushin'/That's what I said/The looser the waistband/The deeper the quicksand/Or so I have read/My baby fits me like a flesh tuxedo/I like to sink her with my pink torpedo."

## CAREER CONSEQUENCES
The longest-running and funniest rock gag ever. Watch out for twentieth anniversary material a-plenty in 2004.

# STEVIE V

## 'Dirty Cash (Money Talks)'
From *The Adventures Of Stevie V* (1990, Mercury)

## STYLE
Grooving dance funk fleshed out with Latino beats and groovy sax.

## THE SORDID DETAILS
The British producer and mixer had an eclectic palate and attempted to meld elements of hip hop, house and '70s disco together with various female vocals to produce something new and exciting. Sadly, the rest of the world wasn't turned on by such tinkering and never really got with Stevie's flow. His own search for dirty cash via music never quite made the grade, despite the fact that the song's lyrics made it clear that whatever it took to get paid would absolutely, definitely, have to be done. Even if it came to using sex as a weapon, which doubtless it often does.

## BEST LINES
"I once had pride/Now that's all behind/I want to get rich quick/I want success/And all that goes with it/And I'm gonna use my sex."

## CAREER CONSEQUENCES
Nothing doing. Stevie V didn't make the grade as a production guru. But who knows? Maybe he made his cash selling used cars in Connecticut!

# THE STOOGES

### 'Cock In My Pocket'
From *Studio Sessions* (Pilot, 1996)

## ✗ STYLE
Raw hard rock mixed with a definite appreciative nod toward old-time rock'n'roll.

## ✗ THE SORDID DETAILS
'Cock Out Of My Pocket' may have been more appropriate for James Osterberg, given his propensity for showing his sizeable manhood pretty much at the drop of a hat. No matter, 'Cock In My Pocket' shows The Stooges firing on all cylinders, but adding a rock'n'roll swing to their repertoire that was often lost in their bulldozing sludge rock approach. Rattling keyboards drive the number as Iggy reflects on the carnal urge going on down below and his straightforward reflections on sex ("I just wanna fuck, I don't want no romance") mirror the music's bad boy malevolence. This song gives credence to the idea that rock'n'roll has to be nasty if it's done right.

## ✗ BEST LINES
"I got my cock in my pocket/And I'm shovin it through your pants/I just want to fuck and I don't want no romance."

## ✗ CAREER CONSEQUENCES
Legendary status has been bestowed on The Stooges for their encapsulation of total rock'n'roll. Songs like this did much to cement that reputation.

# THE STRANGLERS

## 'Peaches'
From *Stranglers IV – Rattus Norvegicus* (United Artists, 1977)

## STYLE
Appropriately organ-heavy take on punk rock that fooled many young and spiky impressionables into believing that this was something exciting, new and revolutionary – then someone came across a Doors album.

## THE SORDID DETAILS
On the surface, The Stranglers did not appear to be types to excite spotty pogoers at the dawn of punk. Members Hugh Cornwell and Jean-Jacques Burnel were science teacher and history graduate respectively, while drummer Jet Black (stand up Brian Duffy!) was already 33 years old when *Rattus...* was released. Credibility rating should have been nil, but soared with the single release of 'Peaches', an everyday tale of wandering along the beach looking at boobs, arses or a combination of the two, depending on how you interpreted the title's fruity analogy.

## BEST LINES
"Why don't you take a look over there/Where?/There/Is she trying to get out of that clitoris?/Liberation for women, that's what I preach."

## CAREER CONSEQUENCES
The song itself seemed to strike a chord with punk's anti-establishment vibes, but the band soon caused outrage among some punk brethren by introducing strippers at a live gig during another musical trip to the gutter called 'Nice'n'Sleazy'. Seems this was playing the sexist card a little too freely. The band didn't give a toss and soon revelled in confounding the movement even further, releasing a cover of the classic Dionne Warwick hit 'Walk On By'. In retrospect The Stranglers' failure to follow the movement's fashion gives them the greatest punk cred of all.

# SUGARHILL GANG

### 'Rapper's Delight'
From *The Sugarhill Gang* (Sugar Hill, 1980)

## STYLE

The original rap tune by the original rap outfit.

## THE SORDID DETAILS

So what if The Sugarhill Gang was a manufactured group featuring three of New Yorks' best local rappers? 'Rapper's Delight' is still one of the all-time great rap tunes and the flow that started the whole show. Eight million sales of a single featuring a style that no-one had heard on record before stand as testament to the phenomenal impact the tune had at the time. And, of course, the colossal influence it had on the future music scene. As if that wasn't enough, it was even daring enough to have its saucy moments, the very best of which is a fun diss of Superman and his lack of sexual prowess that must have made uptight white folks very nervous indeed. A record of genius, no doubt about it.

## BEST LINES

"He may be very sexy or even cute/But he looks like a sucker in his blue and red suit/I said you need a man who's got finesse/And his whole name across his chest/He may be able to fly all through the night/But can he rock a party till the early light?/He can't satisfy you with his little worm/But I can bust you out with my super sperm."

## CAREER CONSEQUENCES

For the band's career, less than stellar. It was all downward trajectory after this monster and the band faded. As for the style? Well, you know the score.

# DONNA SUMMER

## 'Love To Love You Baby'
From *Love To Love You Baby* (Casablanca, 1975)

## STYLE
Genre-defining disco, effortlessly combining a sensual, string-driven feel and dancefloor-filling groove. But why are we talking about Giorgio Moroder's tune when there's that vocal performance to get after?

## THE SORDID DETAILS
Donna Gaines had already served notice of her tendencies toward musical strumpetry by appearing in the travelling cast of full frontal nudity show *Hair*. While in Germany in the early '70s Gaines married Helmut Sommer (hence the stage name) and met producer Giorgio Moroder, which turned out to be a pretty good double whammy for the American. One sixteen-minute disco giant of a tune later Summer was ready to be crowned Queen Of Disco Dirtiness. Her vocal performance was worthy of any hardcore porn star on top of her game as Summer moaned, groaned and ground her way to the song's climax. Never has a record containing no words that could be defined as rude been so utterly, utterly filthy – apart from the Birkin/Gainsbourg effort which this song clearly rips off.

## BEST LINES
"Oooh, aaaah, aaah, oooh," (...*and various combinations thereof*).

## CAREER CONSEQUENCES
Summer will never escape those moans and groans. Despite getting religion, going mainstream and singing 'MacArthur Park' there will always be something of the "nudge, nudge, wink wink" associated with the lady.

# JOHNNIE TAYLOR

## 'Who's Making Love?'
From *Who's Making Love?* (Stax, 1968)

## STYLE
Raunchy, 'Soul Man'-sounding fuel for the funkers.

## THE SORDID DETAILS
Known as "The Philosopher Of Soul", Johnnie Taylor was hailed as a '70s crooner who knew how to get the ladies excited. But his earliest incarnation in the late '60s was as an artist with a much harder edge, fronting up on upbeat songs with tough guitars and hard brass stabs. 'Who's Making Love?', his first Number One, also had a ballsy lyric, which pulled no punches when it came to trying to explain the error of the wayward lover's ways.

## BEST LINES
"Reason why I ask this question/I used to be the same old way/When I decided to straighten up/I found it was a bit too late/Oh, that's when it all happened/Something I never, never dreamed of/Somebody was a-lovin' my old lady/While I was out making love/Somebody was-a lovin' my old lady/While I was out making love/Now who's making love to your old lady?"

## CAREER CONSEQUENCES
Smoothing his style throughout the '70s Taylor still managed a massive hit with 'Disco Lady', but the fire of those early performances had all but died. Taylor himself died of a suspected heart attack in 2000.

# JOHN TRAVOLTA

### 'Greased Lightnin''
From *Grease (Original Soundtrack)* (Polydor, 1978)

## STYLE
Raucous and rowdy doo-woppin' rock'n'roll standard that set the tempo for the huge retro film hit.

## THE SORDID DETAILS
This one's all about context. People forget that despite his dimple, the twinkling eyes and the smile that made little girls burst into tears with sheer pre-pubescent excitement, John Travolta had made his name in Saturday Night Fever, a movie that had its fair share of sex, drugs and rock'n'roll. While his follow-up effort, *Grease*, was clearly more teen-friendly, it still wasn't anodyne, dealing with unwanted pregnancies and sexual awakening in a fairly candid fashion. For Travolta to be talking about the motor of his dreams as "a pussy wagon" might have gone over the heads of the little girls, but to the lads reaching puberty it was a sure sign that this was more on-the-edge than gullible parents could have imagined.

## BEST LINES
"With new pistons, plugs and shocks I can get off my rocks/You know that I ain't braggin' she's a real pussy wagon/ Greased Lightnin'."

## CAREER CONSEQUENCES
Travolta's slicked-back greaser performance of the song in the movie served to confirm him as one of the most bankable stars in Hollywood and the one most women "definitely would".

# THROBBING GRISTLE

## 'Something Came Over Me'
From *Mission Of Dead Souls* (Mute, 1981)

## STYLE

Dark and throbbing electronica, which given the subject matter seems
entirely appropriate.

## THE SORDID DETAILS

Throbbing Gristle all but invented industrial music in the UK, an anti-
melody and highly adventurous musical artform that delved into the
darker recesses of the human soul and attempted to reflect what it found
there in the mechanical noise that dominated the band's sound. Of
course such earnest work attracted the attentions of glum sixth formers
everywhere, who presumably found some light relief in the
masturbatory musings of 'Something Came Over Me'. Perhaps even
jerking off was seen as an artistic statement at the time, though it's
doubtful that whoever was washing keyboardist Sleazy Peter
Christopherson's sheets would have agreed. The sleeve to the single
version of the song featured a photo of his semen in water.

## BEST LINES

"Something came over me/Was it white and sticky?"

## CAREER CONSEQUENCES

Writing a song about masturbation would be the least of main man
Genesis P.Orridge's worries, given that he is currently in exile from his
native England "following a lifestyle attack by the British Establishment
in 1991". Still, it's not all doom and gloom (apart from on his records).
Genesis did win substantial damages from producer Rick Rubin after
falling from a second storey window at his house to escape a fire.

# TLC

### 'Red Light Special'
From *CrazySexyCool* (La Face, 1994)

## STYLE

Silky smooth smutfest from the R'n'B trio guaranteed to pop the buttons on the pants of any men in the vicinity of the CD player. Could be useful for ladies who are in the mood. And for jeans manufacturers.

## THE SORDID DETAILS

Their 1992 debut album, *Ooooooh On The TLC Tip*, focused on fun R'n'B and hip hop grooves. Two years later CrazySexyCool showed the three TLC girls – T-Boz, Chilli and the late, lamented Left Eye – were suddenly all grown up and ready to talk about doing the do. Written by '90s production king Babyface, 'Red Light Special' leaves little to the imagination, but comes over as both sultry and sleazy, thanks to T-Boz' extraordinarily breathy vocal and the non-committal use of the word "it" (see below). It is entirely possible that babies have been conceived to this very song.

## BEST LINES

"Take a good look at it, look at it now/Might be the last time you'll have a go round/I'll let you touch it if you'd like to go down/I'll let you go further if you take the southern route."

## CAREER CONSEQUENCES

Established TLC as women as opposed to girls. And women who were in control, at that. Just ask American footballer Andre Rison, then boyfriend of Left Eye, whose house was burnt down in a "domestic" just before the release of *CrazySexyCool*. Doubtless the flames lapping at Rison's house weren't exactly the kind of red light he thought the song was referring to.

# TOOL

### 'Jerk-Off'
From *Opiate* (1992)

## STYLE

Grinding alternative metal mixed with a definite pretension toward art. The results are oddly addictive.

## THE SORDID DETAILS

An unlikely success story. A runty-looking frontman singing songs of despair and hatred, a sound that's frankly disturbing and an attitude to its audience that said nothing for the band's PR skills. And yet Tool was taken to America's rock bosom and showered with both praise and Number One albums. 'Jerk-Off' sums up their user-unfriendly approach perfectly, but it also has an undeniable musical presence that can't be ignored. Vocalist Maynard James Keenan (oh yes, they're pretentious too) puts every ounce of vitriol into this tune and throws a curveball at the end by announcing that he'd like to have sex with the object of his utter disdain. Nasty, but compelling.

## BEST LINES

"I should kick you, beat you, fuck you/And then shoot you in your fucking head."

## CAREER CONSEQUENCES

Tool have escaped the post-grunge fallout admirably and proved it by sending third album proper *Lateralus* to Number One on the US album charts in 2001.

# TOO SHORT

### 'Blowjob Betty'
From *Get In Where You Fit In* (Jive, 1993)

##  STYLE

Slow and low, bass-heavy rap specifically designed for ladies who are very proud of their bottoms and care to show them off in hot pants on a variety of music promotional videos.

## THE SORDID DETAILS

Sordid indeed. Original West Coast rapper Todd Shaw is caught mid-career here, recounting a sorry tale of how he is responsible for the death of a girl called Blowjob Betty. As her name suggests, our heroine is depicted as a woman who is free with her favours and gets her "cum-uppance" in a novel and, frankly, unbelievable way. In typical rap braggadocio style, Too Short claims to have delivered the fatal blow to Blowjob, who dies choking on sperm in the windpipe. Pretty it is not.

## BEST LINES

"But that next day I read this story/A young girl died just last night/She choked on sperm in her windpipe/It was on her face, her neck and chest/And we're sorry to say there's no suspect/When I saw that my brain clicked/I bust a nut and killed a bitch."

## CAREER CONSEQUENCES

Well, Too Short is still pumping the albums out, still delivering tales about sex and bitches. So it's not as if the Moral Majority got rid of him, is it? Of course the days of being Number One West Coast boy are long gone, but the man still gets respect for being one of the originals – and one of the rudest rappers on record.

# X TERENCE TRENT D'ARBY

## 'Supermodel Sandwich w/Cheese'
From *Terence Trent D'Arby's Vibrator* (Columbia, 1995)

## X STYLE

Maudlin soul that's in total contrast to the supposed excitement of having it off with two models at the same time.

## X THE SORDID DETAILS

Terence Trent D'Arby has a voice that quite rightly saw him hailed as the saviour of music when he first appeared in 1987. But the weight of his pretensions immediately weighed him down on second album *Neither Fish Nor Flesh* and the precociously talented singer's star has steadily fallen ever since. It was almost as if he willfully threw away his success. This 1995 song isn't much to write home about on a musical front. In fact, the only thing about it that can raise any enthusiasm is the idea of a threesome – and TTD's hardly going out on a limb in sexual fantasy terms there, is he? Still, better than writing about fish, eh?

## X BEST LINES

"I'm a guy so I sigh/But you ain't shy/Besta, besta, best of all you're bi bi bi."

## X CAREER CONSEQUENCES

There have been rumours of another album, *The Solar Return Of Terence Trent D'Arby*, since 1999. So far, though, nothing from pop's prince of the perverse.

# TRICK DADDY (FEATURING TRINA)

'Nann Nigga'
From *www.thug.com* (Warlock, 1998)

##  STYLE

Really sleazy rap tune with a call and response duet that owes precisely nothing to Sonny and Cher.

##  THE SORDID DETAILS

Trick Daddy Dollars, to give him his full name, is a South Florida producer and rapper who's yet to make the big breakthrough, though judging by this groove there's no reason why he shouldn't. Joined by Trina (who certainly sounds like she'd be good fun to spend some time with), this is an unoriginal bragging affair lifted out of the ordinary by some spirited performances by Trick and Trina and a sparse yet warm groove with woofer-wafting bass.

##  BEST LINES

"Nigga you don't know nann hoe uh-uh/That don' tried all types of shit/Who quick to deep throat the dick/And let another bitch straight lick the clit/Now you don't know nann hoe uh-uh/That'll keep it wet like me/Make it come back to back like me/Lick a nigga nut sack like me." *(Which really is very nice of Trina.)*

##  CAREER CONSEQUENCES

Still pushing the thug lifestyle at a time when it's not as hip to do so, The Trickster is keepin' it real!

# TRIPLE SIX MAFIA

## 'Long And Hard (Original Version)'
From *Club Memphis Underground Volume 2* (Smoked Out, 1999)

## STYLE
Slow and low groove that sounds for a second or two like it could be about something romantic. Fat chance.

## THE SORDID DETAILS
Even in a world of super-cussin' rap Triple Six Mafia have some exceedingly dirty mouths. Let's hope their mothers haven't heard this song about sucking on the pipe (and we're not talking crack here) because it really is very rude indeed. The word "enlightened" could not be used to describe this everyday tale of young and testosterone-filled males demanding oral sex from friendly young girls. But then again this Tennessee crew would surely get the ache if you levelled that one at them anyway. So let's just straighten things out so everyone knows what's going on here, OK? These guys like getting their dicks sucked – a lot.

## BEST LINES
"Let's meet at six o'clock/You gotta lotta pants to rock/And with them triple six niggaz there is no holds barred/You gotta swallow the dick long and hard."

## CAREER CONSEQUENCES
As you may well be aware, there's a market for this X-rated stuff, which may account for the album from which 'Long And Hard' is taken going gold.

# T-SPOON

## 'Sex On The Beach'
From *The Hit Collection* (Remixed Records, 1997)

##  STYLE

Super-cheesy Euro disco with ragga filling for added "authenticity".

## THE SORDID DETAILS

"A household name on the Dutch music scene," announces T-Spoon's official website breathlessly. And indeed they are. Elsewhere, however, the Spoon are only known for their "liberal as only the Dutch can be" monster hit 'Sex On The Beach', which as you might expect became an anthem for all of Europe's 18–30s on holiday in 1997. The band can't believe it wasn't played by the BBC until after midnight. "I mean, whatsch wrong with these crayshy English guysh?" asked Spoon mainman Remy De Groot. You really should try getting it played in America, pal.

## BEST LINES

"She said her name was Cindy/Would you like a drink of me?/Bikini on the left, daiquiri on the right/Come and give me lovin' all through the night."

## CAREER CONSEQUENCES

They said they're a household name on the Dutch music scene. Weren't you listening?

# 2 LIVE CREW

## 'Me So Horny'
From *As Nasty As They Wanna Be* (Luke, 1989)

## STYLE
Musical fusion of Miami base and preliminary hip hop, all completely overshadowed by the dirty, filthy, obscene lyrics.

## THE SORDID DETAILS
2 Live Crew is probably the most notorious rap group ever, purely because of their X-rated lyrical content. Given that they have operated in a field littered with blokes bragging in graphic detail about their sexual escapades, this is no mean feat. "Credit" for the Crew goes to Florida promoter and record label owner Luther Campbell, who conceived of an outrageous, sex-obsessed band in 1985. 'Me Want Some Pussy' from 1986's *Is What We Are* set the tone for the band's straight-talking lyrical stance, but 'Me So Horny' was the song that really brought the band (and their collective hard-ons) to the public conscience.

## BEST LINES
"You said it yourself, you like it like I do/Put your lips on my dick, and suck my asshole too/I'm a freak in heat, a dog without warning/My appetite is sex, 'cause me so horny."

## CAREER CONSEQUENCES
Unsurprisingly the band got embroiled in a running battle with the PMRC, being held up as the prime example of the filth that was being peddled to "our kids" in the name of entertainment. And to be fair, they had a point. In the end people just got bored of the controversy and while the Crew were still at it in the new millennium, no-one much cared any more.

# 2PAC

## 'Thug Passion'
From *All Eyez On Me* (Death Row, 1996)

### ✖ STYLE
Classic West Coast gangsta rap with the trademark reedy synth lines and thick bass that allows 2Pac to deliver a strutting paean to the thug life that eventually cost him his life.

### ✖ THE SORDID DETAILS
While Tupac Shakur was perfectly capable of writing a sensitive lyric, when the mood took him he was easily as louche and base as any of his fellow rappers. This straightforward lyrical idea sees him biggin' up his lifestyle (check the obligatory mention of "Chrystal") and clearly enjoying his sexual prowess, which he claims is enhanced by copious amounts of alcohol. Possibly not the way his supporters would like to remember rap's biggest martyr, but the music doesn't lie.

## ✖ BEST LINES
"This drink is guaranteed to get the pussy wet and the dick hard/Now if ya with me pour a glass and drink with a nigga."

### ✖ CAREER CONSEQUENCES
It was this kind of bragging that suddenly got out of hand when it became personal and the "war" between West and East coast rappers exploded. Dissin' of rivals in such a particularly overt and permanent way proved to be more than some egos could bear and the untimely demise of 2Pac in Vegas was the inevitable consequence.

# UNWRITTEN LAW

## 'Sorry'
From *Unwritten Law* (Interscope, 1998)

## STYLE
Fairly frenetic pop punk that's all a bit too clean and precise to carry this "treat 'em mean, keep 'em keen" lyric.

## THE SORDID DETAILS
This most promiscuous of Californian skate punk bands has already recorded for three different labels in a relatively short career, which may be an indication of the lack of success that's greeted most of their efforts. It's not as if they have much to make them stand out — and even when they write a lyric that has the requisite "angry young men" attributes somehow it just doesn't seem all that convincing. In 'Sorry' vocalist Scott Russo claims he throws the object of his affections on her arse, but somehow you suspect he might have put a pillow on the floor beforehand.

## BEST LINES
"Slow down boy I'm not easy/Don't wanna be a sleazy whore/So I've thrown her to the floor upon that fine butt cheek/And I'm not sorry, no I'm not sorry."

## CAREER CONSEQUENCES
Not much to date. Seeing as skate punk stuff is so hip it's almost amazing that this lot have remained such a secret. What does that tell you?

# VILLAGE PEOPLE

### 'Sex Over The Phone'
From *Sex Over The Phone* (Polygram, 1999)

## X STYLE

Ridiculous and camp '80s pop espousing the pleasures of paying for an unmarried mother to talk dirty to you while she does the ironing. Oh, sorry, for someone really hot and sexy and probably wearing something very skimpy to get you off.

## X THE SORDID DETAILS

A blatant attempt by everybody's favourite camp act to whip up some controversy with some frankly limp '80s R'n'B flim flam. Despite the saucy nature of the lyrics and the insertion of some "real life" sex over the phone conversation, if anybody out there is actually able to get turned on by this ludicrous attempt at sleaze, then they deserve a medal. They also need to be restrained for the good of society.

## X BEST LINES

"Hello?/Hello baby, it's me, your fantasy/What's your name?/Who cares? Just care about my body/What do you look like?/Hot. Hot, I'm very hot."

## X CAREER CONSEQUENCES

The Village People bandwagon continues to roll and nothing – whether it's band members leaving or even dying in the case of biker Glenn Hughes – is about to stop the party.

# DINAH WASHINGTON

## 'Big Long Sliding Thing'
From *The Complete Dinah Washington On Mercury Vol. 3*
(1952-54) (Mercury, 1992)

## STYLE

An impossibly sleazy and slow brass intro warms the listener up just nicely for Washington's ultra-knowing delivery.

## THE SORDID DETAILS

If you really think this song's about a trombone, what are you doing reading this book?! With just the seven marriages behind her Ruth Lee Jones must surely be considered something of a world expert on matters horizontal. And this tune finds the legendary Dinah in one of her muckiest moods. Given that her first ever hit was titled 'Evil Gal Blues' it's safe to say that Dinah Washington's take on jazz was always going to revolve around doing the naughty. 'Big Long Sliding Thing' may not contain one dirty word, but it's right up there with the crème de la crème of saucy songs.

## BEST LINES

"He brought his amplifier and he hitched it in my plug/He planked and he plunked it but it just wasn't good enough/'Cos I need my daddy with that big long sliding thing."

## CAREER CONSEQUENCES

Serious-minded jazz critics with beards may have accused her of bad taste in recording songs like this, but that didn't stop Washington from becoming revered as one of the genre's great vocal practitioners, regardless of the dubious song quality of some of her later ballad recordings. Living hard to the last, Washington died at the age of 39 of an accidental overdose of diet pills mixed with alcohol.

# W.A.S.P

## 'Animal (Fuck Like A Beast)'

From *Animal (Fuck Like A Beast)* (Four track EP, Restless, 1983)

## ⊠ STYLE

Over-the-top heavy-metal with a slight touch of glam rock sandwiched in-between the crunching riffs.

## ⊠ THE SORDID DETAILS

Frontman and bassist Blackie Lawless had already had a dry run at rock stardom with a short-lived alliance with The New York Dolls. But on settling in Los Angeles he took the glam tendencies he'd learned and allied them to both a harder sound and more sexual imagery. Putting a topless woman on a rack on stage, throwing raw meat at the audience and recording the song 'Animal (Fuck Like A Beast)' were all calculated moves to attain a certain notoriety, and the plan worked – for a while at least. 'Animal (Fuck Like A Beast)' made headlines because it had the word "fuck" in its elongated, bracketed title and junior metalers fought each other to get on board the W.A.S.P. (that's "We Are Sexual Perverts of course!) bandwagon.

## ⊠ BEST LINES

"I do whatever I want to, to ya/I'll nail your ass to the sheets/A pelvic thrust and the sweat starts to sting ya/I fuck like a beast."

## ⊠ CAREER CONSEQUENCES

If W.A.S.P. had continued in their schlock horror vein, then maybe they could have become Alice Cooper's younger brother. As it was the band's music veered into the commercial, guitarist Chris Holmes veered into alcoholism and Lawless wrote a totally useless rock opera. W.A.S.P. are still making albums, though who's listening to them is a mystery up there with anything from Roswell.

# ETHEL WATERS

### 'Organ Grinder Blues'
From *The Chronological Ethel Waters: 1926-1929*
(French Classics, 1974)

## STYLE
Rude and raw blues that leaves next to nothing to the listener's imagination.

## THE SORDID DETAILS
Ethel Waters may well have recorded the blatantly obscene 'Organ Grinder Blues', but her talents and career extended way beyond the titillating lyrics and wild music of jump blues. Born in Pennsylvania, married at the age of 13 and originally billed in the tent shows where she started her career as "Sweet Mama Stringbean", Waters started out as a blues artist, then quickly developed her style to include jazz and eventually pop – and even made a name for herself as a dramatic actress. But if you're reading this book you'll be most impressed by this lascivious little Clarence Williams number, recorded on August 23, 1928 in New York.

## BEST LINES
"Grind it north, south, grind east or west/But when you grind it slow that's when I like it best/Organ grinder don't tell me you're through/'Cos if you want an intermission mama's gonna grind a little while for you."

## CAREER CONSEQUENCES
Although it's easy to see where the inspiration to sing 'Organ Grinder Blues' came from (Waters grew up in a red light district), Ethel's 1957 conversion to Christianity doubtless meant that this would not be one of her favourite recordings.

 **WEEN**

## 'She Fucks Me'
From *Paintin' The Town Brown — Ween Live '90–'98*
(Mushroom, 1999)

##  STYLE

Bizarrely mellow, almost soppy little country-tinged ballad, somewhat at odds with the matter-of-factness of the fucking.

##  THE SORDID DETAILS

Described by some as "the ultimate cosmic goof of the alternative rock era" and by others as "total losers", Ween were formed by 14-year-olds Mickey Melchiondo and Aaron Freeman in New (No?) Hope, Pennsylvania, back in 1984. Making a virtue of drunkenness, there seems very little reason for Ween ever to have existed except for their own amusement. But exist they do. The juxtaposition of a certain warped tenderness in this song and a pretty rude word repeated quite a lot is rather fitting. 1996 was obviously a very strange year.

##  BEST LINES

"She's in my arms, she's in my heart, yeah/Pins and needles up and down my spine/We're together, she really digs me now/She fucks me, she fucks me/She fucks me."

##  CAREER CONSEQUENCES

What career? Ween is a labour of love that by its very definition appears incapable of following a traditional career trajectory. Believe me, saying "fuck" in a song is the least of this band's worries when lined up next to their self-proclaimed "anthem" 'Poopship Destroyer'.

# BARRY WHITE

## 'It's Ecstasy When You Lay Down Next To Me'
From *Barry White Sings For Someone You Love* (A&M, 1977)

## STYLE

Bass-throbbing disco with the lushest of strings overlaid for that final push over the satin-sheeted love cliff.

## THE SORDID DETAILS

Barry White, as everybody knows, is The Walrus of Love, a big hunk of flesh waving a silk handkerchief, promising nights of unremitting naughtiness and with a voice which appears able to charm the knickers from the thighs of women aged 16 to 60. White also provides proof positive that you don't actually have to say something dirty during a song to make it sound positively filthy. As rude records go, 'It's Ecstasy...' takes some beating.

## BEST LINES

**"Livin' in ecstasy, well, when you're layin' down next to me/Ooh! ooh! eeh, ecstasy, when you're layin' here with me, uh-huh."**

## CAREER CONSEQUENCES

The Lover Man continues to prosper, safe in the knowledge that countless couples will still happily tell him that their babies were made under the influence of Barry White.

# WINGS

### 'Hi Hi Hi'
From *Wings Greatest* (EMI, 1978)

## STYLE

Rollicking rock'n'roll from the king of the cheery grin and the ever-skyward-pointing thumbs.

## THE SORDID DETAILS

First seen on the triple *Wings Over America* and later issued in studio form on *Wings Greatest*, this is about the closest you get to hearing the oh-so-romantic Macca getting a rocket in his pocket. A silly little tale of getting wasted and having sex, the tune fair belts along (presumably as Macca works himself into a frenzy about the pleasures to come) as our mop-top-turned-mullet-man starts getting all obtuse, referring to his schlong as his polygon. They did that kind of thing in the '70s, you know. A throwaway rock'n'roller which is clearly the sound of a man enjoying himself...and there's nothing wrong with that now, is there?

## BEST LINES

"Well, well take off your face, recover from the trip you've been on/I want you to lie on the bed, get you ready for my polygon/I'm gonna do it to you, gonna do ya sweet banana/You'll never give up/Yes and like a rabbit, gonna grab it, gonna do it till the night is done."

## CAREER CONSEQUENCES

Paul McCartney enjoyed this one minor hit, before disappearing back into the obscurity from whence he came. Hang on, that's not quite right, is it?

# WOLFSBANE

### 'Totally Nude'
From *All Hell's Breaking Loose Down At Little Kathy Wilson's Place* (Def American, 1990)

## STYLE

Kinetic heavy-metal marrying undoubted leadweight credentials with a dumb and proud party attitude.

## THE SORDID DETAILS

Wolfsbane were British rock press darlings throughout their short but explosive career, but were utterly unable to turn such goodwill into record sales worth talking about. Signed by Yankee production guru Rick Rubin to the Def American label for 1989's *Live Fast, Die Fast* album, it was only on the following year's six-track EP *All Hell's Breaking Loose…* that the band's undoubted power was really heard on record. Of course there was humour too, from the filthy mouth of Van Halen-influenced frontman Blaze Bayley, as 'Totally Nude' proves.

## BEST LINES

"Two pounds only The Tavern In The Town would like you to welcome on stage, utterly naked and wearing just shoes, the lovely Sabrina." (All delivered as a rap in a broad Midlands brogue.)

## CAREER CONSEQUENCES

British metal fans had never traditionally trusted too much showmanship from their own acts and Bayley was eventually forced to retreat to a more conventional style as the singer in Iron Maiden. Wolfsbane promptly imploded.

# WRECKX-N-EFFECT

## 'Rump Shaker'
From *Hard Or Smooth* (MCA,1992)

## STYLE

Big flapping bass drum mixes with a persuasive horn riff as the band lay down their excitement over jiggling butt cheeks in exemplary fashion.

## THE SORDID DETAILS

Featuring the talents of Markell Riley, brother of superstar producer Teddy Riley, Wreckx-n-Effect had their one moment in the sun thanks to the rude riding 'Rump Shaker' from their second album *Hard Or Smooth*, a homage to the ladies who were making a big thing (often quite literally) of swinging their butts to the beat. Of course with Teddy Riley producing, mixing, playing a variety of instruments on the album and even rapping on 'Rump Shaker', it was no surprise that the track sounded like a ready-made classic. And the video which accompanied the song, featuring a bunch of beautiful women following the band's instructions on what exactly to do with the booty, made possibly even more of an impression than the track itself.

## BEST LINES

"Shake it, shake it, shake it now shake it/She can spend every birthday butt naked/Body is soft, makin me wanna squish her/More just than a game, a rumper like a sub-woofer/Shake it to the left, shake it to the right/I don't mind stickin' it to her every single night..."

## CAREER CONSEQUENCES

The band resurfaced in 1996 with another album, but this was strictly a one-off deal as far as the paying public was concerned and the act faded to obscurity. Teddy Riley, of course, went on to become one of the most influential producers in black music.

# YEAH YEAH YEAHS

**Bang**
From *Master* (Shifty, 2001)

## STYLE
Quirky cross between new-style blues and old-style new wave. These New Yorkers, they're mad you know...

## THE SORDID DETAILS
This Brooklyn pop punk three piece have a lot to live up to, having been hyped to buggery on the back of opening slots for New York scenesters The Strokes and critics' darlings The White Stripes, not to mention a UK tour with The Jon Spencer Blues Explosion. Their five-track debut sounds like it's trying a little bit too hard to be in there by being "out there", but there's no doubt that while Karen O wouldn't recognise real singing if it bit her on the arse, the much repeated chorus line of "As a fuck, son, you suck" is very nearly certified genius.

## BEST LINES
"Take a swallow as I spit baby/As a fuck, son, you suck."
(Repeated just the eight times each chorus)

## CAREER CONSEQUENCES
Nobody knows. Clearly, they're not going to be voted "Most Likely To..." by that True Love Waits lot.

# FRANK ZAPPA

### 'Why Does It Hurt When I Pee?'
From *Joe's Garage Act I* (Zappa Records, 1979)

## STYLE
Fuzzed-up, mid-paced jazz rock with a sense of impending doom, which perfectly captures the singer's dawning realisation that he's gone caught something really bad!

## THE SORDID DETAILS
Zappa's 1979 narrative of the trials and tribulations of moving from naïve garage band to thoroughly corrupted rock pigs is an absolute gem. Full of sardonic wit and an unblinking determination to show rock's seedy underbelly, the lyrics are so clever, funny and sad that you can almost forget the sheer quality of the music spilling out of your speakers. With a bunch of top line players, including guitarist Warren Cucurullo and drummer Vinnie Colaiuta, the playing is tighter than such supposedly stoopid subject matter has a right to expect.

## BEST LINES
"My balls feel like a pair of maracas." (x two)

## CAREER CONSEQUENCES
A bit of a redundant question for Zappa. Let's face it, Frank's schtick has never relied on anything other than a loyal fanbase of burnouts, freaks and hippies. Possibly a touch more commercial than much of his work, *Joe's Garage* charted a full thirty-one places behind its predecessor *Sheik Yerbouti* in the UK at 62 and six slots behind the US chart showing of 21. Work that one out if you can...

# ROB ZOMBIE

## 'The Ballad Of Resurrection Joe And Rosa Whore'
From *Hellbilly Deluxe* (Geffen, 1998)

## STYLE
Psychotic industrialised heavy rock punctuated with plenty of samples. In this case it's birds singing, no less!

## THE SORDID DETAILS
Crude credentials in place via a stint as art director of a porno mag, Robert Cummings mutated into Rob Zombie via White Zombie, an over-the-top distillation of gore movies and comic books set to metal music. Whether the intention was to sound genuinely frightening or not, White Zombie always seemed too arch to be real, and Zombie's first solo album followed the exact same path. Even dark and depressing lyrics such as on 'The Ballad...' (and of course it's not a ballad!) somehow seem written with the express intent of shocking someone or other. The guy just doesn't seem that fucked up. File under "Fun (warped)".

## BEST LINES
"She wants some more sweet Rosa Whore/She wants some more sweet Rosa Whore/I say 'hell is love.' you say I must suffer/She's a motherfucker/Resurrect me."

## CAREER CONSEQUENCES
Mr Zombie is still lauded as a true metal innovator and has expanded his horizons to include animation and film directing, even if his first effort at the latter art form, *House Of 1000 Corpses*, was rejected by Universal, who originally funded the venture.

# X THE 10 RUDEST ALBUM SLEEVES EVER

# SCORPIONS

## *Lovedrive*
*(Harvest, 1979)*

A handsome, well-groomed couple sit in the back of an expensive-looking motor. They are the very picture of moneyed elegance. So why does the woman have the top of her dress pulled down? And why, exactly, is her boob connected to the man's hand by a huge glob of stringy chewing gum?

# OHIO PLAYERS

## *Fire*
*(Mercury, 1975)*

The Ohio Players gained a reputation for their super-glamourous gatefold sleeves throughout the '70s and Fire is the finest example. A hard-bodied, sweat-drenched girl is wrapped up in an enormous firehose. OK, we get it. The girl is "hot" and she needs a good "hose" to help put the flames out.

# THE JIMI HENDRIX EXPERIENCE

## *Electric Ladyland*
*(Track, 1968)*

Nineteen young ladies are rounded up off the streets of London to pose for Jimi Hendrix' latest magnum opus. They are paid a fiver each to go topless. Then they are incentivized with another two pounds to get their knickers down. The devilish plan works and voilà, great art is born.

# THE WILDHEARTS

## *Phuq*
*(eastwest, 1995)*

What's so risqué about a purple velvet sleeve? Nothing at all. But check out the inner sleeve designs and you'll see what all the fuss is about. Bizarre line drawings of troll-like creatures abound and in one particular drawing one older troll is getting head from a very young one. The sleeve was banned in England, but allowed in Japan.

## ROXY MUSIC

### *Country Life*
*(Island, 1974)*

The little boys certainly understood. Next to the underwear section in the Grattan catalogue, this was the sexiest shot known to juveniles in the '70s. Two odd but alluring German girls are photographed in the bushes. Both are wearing see-through knickers with pubic hair clearly visible. One is holding her own breasts. Do you really need to know any more?

 ## NASHVILLE PUSSY

### *Let Them Eat Pussy*
*(Polygram, 1998)*

The band's two ultra rock'n'roll chicks are shot from below with two male heads being thrust into their genital areas. The album is called Let Them Eat Pussy. This is a literal interpretation.

## QUEEN

### *Jazz*
*(EMI, 1978)*

OK, it's not the cover that's saucy, but rather the free poster that was given away with the album, which just happened to feature an all-women nude bicycle race to highlight the double A-sided single 'Fat Bottomed Girls'/'Bicycle Race'. And why isn't it an Olympic sport now?

## WHITESNAKE

### *Love Hunter*
*(United Artists, 1979)*

Un-reconstructed cock rockers who made a name for themselves with bluesy rock and rudey sleeves. Love Hunter featured a painting of a naked woman riding an enormous and slightly scary snake. I think we all know what that meant...

## 2 LIVE CREW

### As Nasty As They Wanna Be

*(Luke, 1989)*

Four of the best backsides available wearing barely visible thongs lined up on the beach with the four band members lying on the sand and shot between the girls' spread legs. It's not high art, but it's definitely rude.

## GUNS N' ROSES

### Appetite For Destruction

*(Geffen, 1987)*

The original sleeve features a painting titled Mechanical Rape, where a vicious beast is towering over a helpless girl with her top ripped down. Such graphic imagery, even in a cartoonish painting, proved too much for many and the sleeve was banned in many territories.

216

## COPYRIGHT INFORMATION

Rodney Carrington. 'Magic Roundabout' by Jasper Carrot (DJM, 1975): *Comp/Auth: Jasper Carrot.* UK Owner: Chrysalis Records Ltd. 'Banana In Your Fruit Basket' from *Banana In Your Fruit Basket* by Bo Carter (Yazoo, 1978): *Comp/Auth: Armenter Chatmon.* UK Owner: Columbia Music Publishing Co. 'Did I Shave My Legs For This?' from *Did I Shave My Legs For This?* By Deana Carter (Capitol Nashville, 1995): *Comp/Auth: Deana Carter, Rhonda Hart.* UK Owner: Universal Music Publishing. 'Daddy Should Have Stayed In High School' from *Cheap Trick* by Cheap Trick (Epic, 1977): *Comp/Auth: Rick Nielsen.* UK Owner: Sony/ATV Music Publishing. 'Chocolate Salty Balls (PS I Love You) by Chef from *Chef Aid: The South Park Album* (Columbia, 1998): *Comp/Auth: Trey Parker.* UK Owner: Warner Chappell Music. 'Fucking In Slow Motion' from *Born Again Anti Christian* by Christian Death (Cleopatra, 2001): *Comp/Auth: Valor, Maitri.* UK Owner: Abstract Sounds Ltd. 'Group Sex' from *Group Sex* by Circle Jerks (Epitaph, 1980): *Comp/Auth: Jeff Pierce, Greg Hetson, Keith Leher, Keith Morris, Roger Rogerson.* UK Owner: Rondor Music Ltd. 'Cum Stains On My Pillow' from *XXX Underground* by David Allan Coe (Bootleg, 1980): *Comp/Auth: David Coe.* UK Owner: Leosong Copyright Service Ltd. 'Don't Go Home With Your Hard On' from *Death Of A Ladies' Man* by Leonard Cohen (Warner Bros, 1977): *Comp/Auth: Leonard Cohen, Phil Spector.* UK Owner: Sony/ATV Music Publishing. 'I Wanna Sex You Up' from *CMB* by Color Me Badd (Giant, 1991): *Comp/Auth: Bryan Abrams, Mark Calderon, Samuel Watters, Kevin Thornton, Elliott Straite.* UK Owner: EMI Songs Ltd. 'Fuck Off' from *The Electric Chairs* by Wayne County (Safari French Version, 1978): *Comp/Auth: Vernoy Rogers.* UK Owner: Big Game Music Ltd. 'One Hour Mama' from *I Can't Quit That Man* by Ida Cox (Affinity, 1939) *Comp/Auth: Porter Grainger.* UK Owner: Francis Day Hunter Ltd. 'Can Your Pussy Do The Dog?' from *A Date With Elvis* by The Cramps (New Rose, 1986): *Comp/Auth: Ivy Rorschach, Lux Interior.* UK Owner: Windswept Music (London) Ltd. 'Lollipop Porn' from *The Gift of Game* by Crazy Town (Sony, 1999): *Comp/Auth: Bret Mazur, Seth Binzer, Nicole Larenzo.* UK Owner: EMI Music Publishing. 'Too Drunk To Fuck' from *Give Me Convenience Or Give Me Death* by Dead Kennedys (Alternative Tentacles, 1987): *Comp/Auth: Jello Biafra.* UK Owner: Bug Music Ltd. 'Patricia The Stripper' from *Spanish Train And Other Stories* by Chris De Burgh (A&M, 1976): *Comp/Auth: Chris De Burgh.* UK Owner: Chrysalis Music Ltd. 'Buddy' from *3 Feet High And Rising* by De La Soul (Big Life, 1989): *Comp/Auth: Paul Huston, Kelvin Mercer, David Jolicoeur.* UK Owner: EMI United Partnership Ltd. 'Sucking My Love' from *Lightning To The Nations* by Diamond Head (Fan Club, 1981): *Comp/Auth: Brain Tatler, Sean Harris.* UK Owner: Zomba Music Publishers Ltd. 'I Touch Myself' from *Divinyls* by Divinyls (Virgin, 1990): *Comp/Auth: Billy Steinberg, Tom Kelly, Christina Amphlett, Mark McEntee.* UK Owner: Sony Music Publishing. 'Ass'n'Titties' by DJ Assault (Assault Rifle, 1996): *Comp/Auth: Ade Mainor, Craig Adams.* UK Owner: Electrofunk Ltd. 'Some Bomb Azz Pussy' from *Dogg Food* by Tha Dogg Pound (Death Row, 1995): *Comp/Auth: Delmar Arnaud, Ricardo Brown, Calvin Broadus, Darrell Daniels, Chris Boden.* UK Owner: Warner Chappell Music. 'Diggin' My Potatoes' by Lonnie Donegan (1954, Decca): *Comp/Auth: Ernest Lawler.* UK Owner: Universal MCA Music Ltd. 'The End' from *The Doors* by The Doors (Elektra, 1967): *Comp/Auth: Raymond Manzarek, Jim Morrison, John Densmore, Robert Krieger.* UK Owner: Rondor Music (London) Ltd. 'Too Much Sex (Too Little Jesus)' from *Pizza Deliverance* by Drive-By Truckers (Ghost Meat, 1999): *Comp/Auth: Patterson Hood.* UK Owner: Soul Dump Music. 'Billericay Dickie' from *New Boots And Panties* by Ian Dury and the Blockheads (Stiff, 1977): *Comp/Auth: Stephen Nugent, Ian Dury, Chaz Jankel.* UK Owner: Blackhill Music Ltd. 'Deep' from *Walthamstow* by East 17 (London, 1993): *Comp/Auth: Anthony Mortimer.* UK Owner: Universal Music Publishing Ltd. 'Keep Pimpin'' from *Tha Hall Of Game* by E-40 (Jive, 1996): *Comp/Auth: Earl Stevens, Marvin Whitemon, Daniel Stevens.* UK Owner: Zomba Music Publishing Ltd. 'My Name Is' from *The Slim Shady LP* by Eminem (Interscope, 1999):

*Comp/Auth: M Mathers, Dr Dre. UK Owner: Chrysalis Music Ltd.* 'Whatta Man' by En Vogue (with Salt'n'Pepa) from *Funky Divas* (EastWest, 1993): *Comp/Auth: Cheryl James, Herby Azor, Dave Crawford. UK Owner: Rondor Music (London) Ltd.* 'Why D'Ya Do It?' from *Broken English* by Marianne Faithfull (Island, 1979): *Comp/Auth: Joe Mavety, Marianne Faithful, Steve York, Terry Stannard, Barry Reynolds, John H Williams. UK Owner: Warner Chappell Music.* 'Fucking In Heaven' from *You?ve Come A Long Way Baby* by Fatboy Slim (Skint Records, 1998): *Comp/Auth: Norman Cook. UK Owner: Universal Music Ltd.* 'My Pregnant Head (Labia In The Sunlight' from *Transmissions From The Satellite Heart* by The Flaming Lips (Warner Brothers, 1993): *Comp/Auth: Wayne Coyne, Steven Dzozd, Michael Ivins, Ronald Jones. UK Owner: EMI Music Publishing.* 'With My Little Ukelele In My Hand' from *Formby On Film, Volume 2* by George Formby (Sounds On CD, 1985): *Comp/Auth: Jack Cottrell. UK Owner: Campbell Connelly and Co.* 'Relax' from *Welcome To The Pleasure Dome* by Frankie Goes To Hollywood (ZTT, 1984): *Comp/Auth: William Johnson, Mark O' Toole, Peter Gill. UK Owner: Perfect Songs Ltd.* 'Boobs A Lot' from *The Fugs First Album* by The Fugs (Fantasy, 1965): *Comp/Auth: Steve Weber. UK Owner: ESP-Dick (USA) Ltd.* 'Pussy Ain't Shit' from *Brothas Doobie* by Funkdoobiest (Epic, 1995): *Comp/Auth: Larry Mufferud, Jason Vasquez, Brett Bouldin. UK Owner: Notting Hill Music (UK) Ltd.* 'Je T'Aime (Moi Non Plus)' by Serge Gainsbourg and Jane Birkin (Fontana, 1969): *Comp/Auth: Serge Gainsbourg. UK Owner: Shapiro Bernstein and Co Ltd.* 'After Suck There's Blow' by Gaye Bykers On Acid from *Monsters Of Goth* (Cleopatra, 1997): *Comp/Auth: Ian Hoxley, Kevin Hyde, Ian Reynolds, Richard Horsefall. UK Owner: Maxwood Music Ltd.* 'Let A Ho Be A Ho' from *Grip It! On That Other Level* by Geto Boys (Rap-A-Lot, 1990): *Comp/Auth: Kejuan Muchita. UK Owner: BMG Music Publishing.* 'Cars And Vaginas' by Ginger (Infernal Records, 2001): *Comp/Auth: David Walls.* 'Anything Goes' from *Appetite For Destruction* by Guns N'Roses (Geffen, 1987): *Comp/Auth; Steven Adler, Michael McKagan, Izzy Stradlin, Axl Rose, Slash. UK Owner: Warner Chappell Artemis Music.* 'Kinky Afro' from *Pills'N'Thrills & Bellyaches* by Happy Mondays (Factory, 1990): *Comp/Auth: Shaun Ryder, Paul Ryder, Mark Days, Paul Davis, Gary Whelan. UK Owner: London Music.* 'Suck'n'Swallow' from *Dateless Dudes Club* by Hard-Ons (Waterfront, 1992): *Comp/Auth: Keish De Silva, Peter Black. UK Owner: Universal Music Publishing Ltd.* 'Rid Of Me' from *Rid Of Me* by PJ Harvey (Island, 1993): *Comp/Auth: Polly Harvey. UK Owner: EMI Music Publishing Ltd.* 'Love Comes In Spurts' from *Blank Generation* by Richard Hell and the Voidoids (Stiff, 1976): *Comp/Auth: Richard Hell, Tom Verlaine. UK Owner: Warner Chappell Music.* 'Girls L.G.B.N.A.F.' from *Power* by Ice-T (Sire, 1988): *Comp/Auth: Tracey Marrow, Charles Glenn. UK Owner: Universal MCA Music.* 'Between The Sheets' from *Between The Sheets* by The Isley Brothers (Epic, 1983): *Comp/Auth: Ronald Isley, O?Kelly Isley, Rudolph Isley, Ernest Isley, Marvin Isley, Chris Jasper. UK Owner: EMI Songs Ltd.* 'She Loves My Cock' from *Jackyl* by Jackyl (Geffen, 1992): *Comp/Auth: Jesse Dupree. UK Owner: Universal Island Music Ltd.* 'The Murderers' from *Venni, Vetti, Vecci* by Ja Rule (Def Jam, 1999): *Comp/Auth: Jeffrey Atkins, Irving Lorenzo, Luther Ogletree, R Gill, T Crocker. UK Owner: D J IRV Publishing.* 'Ride'n'Slide' from *Diary Of A Mad Band* by Jodeci (Uptown, 1993): *Comp/Auth: Donald De Grate. UK Owner: EMI Music Publishing Ltd.* 'Meat Balls' from *Complete Works in Chronological Order, Vol. 2 (1936-1937)* by Lil Johnson (Document, 1995): *Comp/Auth: Lil Johnson.* 'Pull Up To The Bumper' from *Nightclubbing* by Grace Jones (Island, 1981): *Comp/Auth: Sly Dunbar, Robbie Shakespeare, Dana Mauno. UK Owner: Universal Island Music Ltd.* 'Big Eight' from *Working Class Ero* by Judge Dread (Trojan, 1973): *Comp/Auth: Alvin Ranglin, Alex Hughes. UK Owner: Hazel Music.* 'Jimbrowski' from *Straight Out The Jungle* by Jungle Brothers (Idler, 1988): *Comp/Auth: Nathaniel Hall, Michael Small. UK Owner: Chelsea Music Publishing Co.* 'Fuck You Blind' from *The Polyfuze Method* by Kid Rock (Continuum, 1993): *Comp/Auth: Robert Richie.*

UK Owner: Notting Hill Music (UK) Ltd. 'Detachable Penis' from *Happy Hour* by King Missile (Atlantic, 1992): *Comp/Auth: John Hall, David Rick, Roger Murdock, Chris Xefos*. UK Owner: *Warner Chappell Music*. 'Coming Soon' by King Sun from *X-Rap - Various Artists* (K-Tel, 1991): *Comp/Auth: Sun Born*. UK Owner: *Warner Chappell Music*. 'He's Just My Size' from *Raunchy Business: Hot Nuts & Lollypops* by Lillian Mae Kirkman (Columbia/Legacy, 1991): *Comp/Auth: Lillie Kirkman*. UK Owner: *Universal MCA Music Ltd*. 'Plaster Caster' from *Love Gun* by KISS (Casablanca, 1977): *Comp/Auth: Gene Simmons*. UK Owner: *Universal Music Publishing*. 'Get Off (You Can Eat A Dick)' from *Spit* by Kittie (Artemis, 1999): *Comp/Auth: Kittie*. UK Owner: *Kittie Inc*. 'A.D.I.D.A.S.' from *Life Is Peachy* by Korn (Immortal/Epic, 1996): *Comp/Auth: Brain Welch, David Silveria, Jonathan Davis, James Shaffer, Reginald Arvizu*. UK Owner: *Warner Chappell Music*. 'Fuck Me I'm A Rock Star' from *360 Degrees* by Latex Generation (One Foot, 1996): *Comp/Auth: Joe Latex, Paulie Latex, Tommy Rockstar*. UK Owner: *OF Music Publishing*. 'The Lemon Song' from *Led Zeppelin II* by Led Zeppelin (Atlantic, 1969): *Comp/Auth: Chester Burnett, John Jones, Robert Plant, Jimmy Page, John Bonham*. UK Owner: *Jewel Music Publishing*. 'King Size Poppa' from : *Tonight?s The Night* by Julia Lee (Charly, 1987): *Comp/Auth: Benny Carter, Paul Vance*. UK Owner: *Anglo-Pic Music Co Ltd*. 'I Think I Got It' from *A Diamond Is A Hard Rock* by Legs Diamond (Phonogram, 1977): *Comp/Auth: Roger Romeo*. UK Owner: *Wally Buddy Music*. 'Big Gay Heart' from *Come On Feel The Lemonheads* by The Lemonheads (Atlantic, 1994): *Comp/Auth: Thomas Morgan, Evan Dando*. UK Owner: *EMI Virgin Music Ltd*. 'Suck My Dick' from *Notorious K.I.M.* by Lil Kim (Atlantic, 2000): *Comp/Auth: Kimberly Jones, R Salas, Carl Thompson, Gary Morgan, Norman Glover*. UK Owner: *Warner Chappell Music*. 'French Kiss' from *French Kiss* by Lil' Louis (Sony, 1989): *Comp/Auth: Marvin Burns, Karlana Johnson*. UK Owner: *London Music*. 'Rocket In My Pocket' from *Waiting For Columbus* by Little Feat (Warner Bros, 1978): *Comp/Auth: Lowell George*. UK Owner: *EMI Music Publishing*. 'Good Golly Miss Molly' from *Little Richard* by Little Richard (RCA Camden, 1958): *Comp/Auth: Robert Blackwell, John Marascallo*. UK Owner: *Prestige Music Ltd*. 'Big Ole Butt' from *Walking With A Panther* by LL Cool J (Def Jam, 1989): *Comp/Auth: Dwanye Simon, James Smith*. UK Owner: *Universal Music Publishing*. 'Spit' from *Wasted In America* by Love/Hate (Columbia, 1992): *Comp/Auth: Chris Rose*. UK Owner: *Sony ATV Publishing Ltd*. 'Area Codes' from *Word Of Mouf* by Ludacris (Def Jam, 2001): *Comp/Auth: Chris Bridges, Phalon Alexander, Nathaniel Hale, William Nichols*. UK Owner: *Warner Chappell Music*. 'Sweaty Betty' from *Beer'n'Sex'n'Chips & Gravy* by6 The Macc Lads (Hectic House, 1985): *Comp/Auth: Tristan O?Neill*. UK Owner: *Link Music Ltd*. 'Where Life Begins' from *Erotica* by Madonna (Maverick, 1992): *Comp/Auth: Madonna Ciccone, Allan Betts*. UK Owner: *Warner Chappell Music*. 'Stripper Vicar' from *Attack Of The Grey Lantern* by Mansun (EMI, 1997): *Comp/Auth: Paul Draper*. UK Owner: *Universal Music Ltd*. 'Sex And Candy' from *Marcy Playground* by Marcy Playground (Capitol, 1997): *Comp/Auth: John Wozniak*. UK Owner: *Warner Chappell Music*. 'Shut The Eff Up (Hoe)' from *Eyes On This* by MC Lyte (First Priority, 1989): *Comp/Auth: Nat Robinson*. UK Owner: *Universal MCA Music Ltd*. 'Get Naked' from *Methods of Mayhem* by Methods Of Mayhem (MCA, 1999): *Comp/Auth: Kimberly Jones, Fred Durst, Tommy Lee*. UK Owner: *EMI Music Publishing*. 'I Want Your Sex' from *Faith* by George Michael (CBS, 1988): *Comp/Auth: George Michael*. UK Owner: *Big Geoff Overseas Ltd*. 'Downloading Porn With Dave' from *The Moldy Peaches* by The Moldy Peaches (Sanctuary, 2001): *Comp/Auth: Adam Green, Kimya Dawson*. 'Bummer' from *Powertrip* by Monster Magnet (A&M, 1998): *Comp/Auth: David Wyndorf*. UK Owner: *Universal Music Publishing Ltd*. 'Let's Go Somewhere And Make Love' from *Sex In The Seventies* by Jackie Moore (Sony, 1995): *Comp/Auth: Jeff Prusan, Bobby Eli*. UK Owner: *Minder Music Ltd*. 'You Oughta Know' from *Jagged Little Pill* by Alanis Morissette (Maverick, 1995): *Comp/Auth: Alanis Morisette, Glen Ballard*. UK

Owner: *Universal MCA Music Ltd.* 'Moan And Groan' from *Return Of The Mack* by Mark Morrison (Atlantic, 1997): *Comp/Auth: Mark Morrison, Billy Moss.* UK Owner: *Perfect Songs Ltd.* 'Capricorn Sister' from *Apple* by Mother Love Bone (Polydor, 1990): *Comp/Auth: Andrew Wood, Stone Gossard, Jeffrey Ament, Gregory Gilmore, Bruce Fairweather.* UK Owner: *Universal Music Publishing Ltd.* 'Leathersex' from *Sexplosion!* by My Life With The Thrill Kill Cult (Interscope, 1991): *Comp/Auth: Groovie Mann, Buzz Mc Coy.* UK Owner: *Spurburn Music.* 'Shake Ya Ass' from *Let's Get Ready* by Mystikal (Jive, 2000): *Comp/Auth: Pharrell Williams, Chad hugo, Mike Tyler.* UK Owner: *EMI Music Publishing Ltd.* 'Piece Of Ass' from *High As Hell* by Nashville Pussy (TVT, 2000): *Comp/Auth: Rick Simms.UK Owner: IQ Music Ltd.* 'Fist Fuck' from *Fixed* by Nine Inch Nails (Nothing/Island, 1992): *Comp/Auth: Trent Reznor.* UK Owner: *Universal MCA Music Ltd.* 'Moist Vagina' from *Singles* Box Set by Nirvana (Geffen, 1995): *Comp/Auth: Kurt Cobain.* UK Owner: *EMI Virgin Music Ltd.* 'Wang Dang Sweet Poontang' from *Double Live Gonzo* by Ted Nugent (Epic, 1978): *Comp/Auth: Ted Nugent.* UK Owner: *IQ Music Ltd.* 'I'd Rather Fuck You' from *Efil4zaggin* by NWA (Ruthless/Priority, 1991): *Comp/Auth: Bootsy Collins, George Clinton, Gary Cooper, Andre Young, Eric Wright, Antoine Carraby.* UK Owner: *Universal Island Music Ltd.* 'Skin Tight' from *Skin Tight* by The Ohio Players (Mercury, 1974): *Comp/Auth: James Williams, Clarence Satchell, Leroy Bonner, Marshall Jones, Ralph Brooks, Marvin Pierce.* UK Owner: *Warner Chappell Music.* 'I Want Pussy' from *Nigga Please* by Ol' Dirty Bastard (Elektra, 1999): *Comp/Auth: Robert Diggs, Russell Jones.UK Owner: Warner Chappell Music.* 'Open Your Box (Hirake)' from *Yoko Ono/Plastic Ono Band* (Rykodisc, 1970): *Comp/Auth: Yoko Ono.* UK Owner: *Ono Music.* 'Let's Get Naked' from *Relish* by Joan Osbourne (Mercury, 1995): *Comp/Auth: Joan Osbourne, Eric Bazilian.* UK Owner: *Universal Music Publishing.* 'We Luv Deez Hoez' from *Stankonia* by Outkast (Arista, 2000): *Comp/Auth: Andre Benjamin, Antwan Patton, Cameron Gipp, Jamahr Williams.* UK Owner: *Chrysalis Music Ltd.* 'Fuck You' from *Fuck You* by Overkill (Megaforce EP, 1987): *Comp/Auth: Robert Ellsworth, Robert Gustafson, Carlo Verni, Lee Kundrat.* UK Owner: *Warner Chappell Music.* 'Bill And Ted's Homosexual Adventure' from *Pile Up* by Pansy Division  (Lookout, 1995): *Comp/Auth: Jon Ginoli.* UK Owner: *Subculture Music.* 'Worker Man' from *Worker Man* by Patra (Epic, 1994): *Comp/Auth: Anthony Kelly, Dorothy Smith, Leroy Romans.* UK owner: *Universal Music Publishing.* 'Fuck The Pain Away' from *Teaches Of Peaches* by Peaches (EFA, 2000): *Comp/Auth: Merrill Nesker.* 'Sex Junkie' from *Beyond The Valley Of 1984* by Plasmatics (Stiff America, 1981): *Comp/Auth: Wes Beech, Rod Swenson.* UK Owner: *Complete Music Ltd.* 'Be My Girl – Sally' from *Outlandos D'Amour* by The Police (A&M, 1978): *Comp/Auth: Gordon Sumner.* UK Owner: *GM Sumner.* 'Beaver Patrol' from *Box Frenzy* by Pop Will Eat Itself (Chapter 22, 1987): *Comp/Auth: Tim Archibalds.* UK Owner: *EMI Songs Ltd.* 'Stranger' from *Presidents Of The United States Of America* by Presidents Of The United States Of America (Columbia, 1995): *Comp/Auth: Chris Ballew, Jason Finn, David Dederer.* UK Owner: *EMI Music Publishing.* 'Jack U Off' from *Controversy* by Prince (Warner Bros, 1981): *Comp/Auth: Prince Rogers-Nelson.* UK Owner: *Universal MCA Music Ltd.* 'Bad Babysitter' from *Princess Superstar Is* by Princess Superstar (K7/Rapster, 2002): *Comp/Auth: Milo Berger, Concetta Kirschner, Erik Meltzer.* UK Owner: *Universal Music Publishing Ltd.* 'Pencil Skirt' from *Different Class* by Pulp (Island, 1995). *Comp/Auth: Jarvis Cocker, Russell Senior, Candida Doyle, Stephen Mackey, Nick Banks, Mark Webber.* UK Owner: *Universal Island Music Ltd.* 'Wicked Inna Bed' from *Rough & Ready Vol. 1* by Shabba Ranks (Epic, 1992): *Comp/Auth: Cleveland Browne, Wycliffe Johnson, Rexton Gordon.* UK Owner: *EMI Music Publishing Ltd.* 'Suck My Kiss' from *BloodSugarSexMagic* by Red Hot Chili Peppers (Warner Bros, 1991): *Comp/Auth: Anthony Keidis, Michael Balzary, John Frusciante, Chad Smith.* UK Owner: *Warner Chappell Music.* 'Give It To Me Raw' from *Extinction Level Event* by Busta Rhymes (Elektra/Asylum, 1998): *Comp/Auth: Kasseem*

Dean, Trevor Smith. *UK Owner: Universal Music Publishing.* 'Essex Girl' from *Motor Driven Bimbo* by Rock Bitch (Steamhammer, 1999): *Compl/Auth: Rockbitch (Group Writers). UK Owner: Warner Chappell Music.* 'Cocksucker Blues' from *Cocksucker Blues* by Rolling Stones (Blank Bootleg, 1977): *Compl/Auth: Mick Jagger, Keith Richards. UK Owner: EMI Music Publishing Ltd.* 'Slut' from *Something/Anything?* By Todd Rundgren (Bearsville, 1972): *Compl/Auth: Todd Rundgren. UK Owner: EMI Music Publishing Ltd.* 'Let's Talk About Sex' from *Blacks' Magic* by Salt 'N' Pepa (Polygram, 1990): *Compl/Auth: Fingerprints. UK Owner: Warner Chappell Music.* 'Don't Make No Promises' from *Animal Magnetism* by Scorpions (Harvest, 1980): *Compl/Auth: Matthias Jabs, Herman Rarebell. UK Owner: BMG Music Publishing Ltd.* 'Friggin' In The Riggin'' from *The Great Rock'n'Roll Swindle* by Sex Pistols (Virgin, 1979): *Compl/Auth: Stephen Jones.* 'Underneath Your Clothes' from *Laundry Service* by Shakira (Sony, 2001): *Compl/Auth: Lester Mendez, Shakira Mebarak. UK Owner: Sony ATV Music Publishing Ltd.* 'Baby Got Back' from *Mack Daddy* by Sir Mix-A-Lot (Def America, 1991): *Compl/Auth: Anthony Ray, Juan Atkins, Doug Craig. UK Owner: EMI Virgin Music Ltd.* 'Swallow' from *Smart* by Sleeper (Indolent, 1995): *Compl/Auth: Louise Wener. UK Owner: Sony Music Publishing Ltd.* 'Treat Her Like A Prostitute' from *The Great Adventures Of Slick Rick* by Slick Rick (Def Jam, 1988): *Compl/Auth: Ricky Walters. UK Owner: Universal Music Publishing Ltd.* 'Empty Bed Blues' from *Incomparable* by Bessie Smith (Columbia River, 1999): *Compl/Auth: J Johnson. UK Owner: EMI Harmonies Ltd.* 'Sex Dwarf' from *Non Stop Erotic Cabaret* by Soft Cell (Sire, 1981): *Compl/Auth: David Ball, Marc Almond. UK Owner: Warner Chappell Music.* 'Big Dumb Sex' from *Louder Than Love* by Soundgarden (A&M, 1989): *Compl/Auth: Chris Connell. UK Owner: Universal MCA Music Ltd.* 'Hoedown' from *Youngest In Charge* by Special Ed (Profile, 1989): *Compl/Auth: Edward Archer, Howard Thompson. UK Owner: Warner Chappell Music Ltd.* 'Big Bottom' from *Music From The Original Motion Picture Soundtrack* by Spinal Tap (Polydor, 1984): *Compl/Auth: Chris Guest, Michael McKean, Ron Reiner, Harry Shearer. UK Owner: EMI Tunes Ltd.* 'Dirty Cash (Money Talks)' from *The Adventures Of Stevie V* by Stevie V (Mercury, 1990): *Compl/Auth: Stephen Vincent, Mick Walsh. UK Owner: Universal MCA Music Ltd.* 'Cock In My Pocket' from *Studio Sessions* by Iggy Pop (Pilot, 1996): *Compl/Auth: Iggy Pop, James Williamson. UK Owner: Bug Music Ltd.* 'Peaches' from *Stranglers IV - Rattus Norvegicus* by The Stranglers (United Artists, 1977): *Compl/Auth: Hugh Cornwall, Jean-Jacques Burnel, Brian Duffy, David Greenfield. UK Owner: Complete Music Ltd.* 'Rapper's Delight' from *The Sugarhill Gang* by The Sugarhill Gang (Sugar Hill, 1980): *Compl/Auth: Nile Rodgers, Bernard Edwards. UK Owner: Warner Chappell Music.* 'Love To Love You Baby' from *Love To Love You Baby* by Donna Summer (Casablanca, 1975): *Compl/Auth: Giorgio Moroder, Pete Bellotte, Donna Summer. UK Owner: Warner Chappell Music.* 'Who's Making Love?' from *Who's Making Love?* by Johnnie Taylor (Stax, 1968): *Compl/Auth: Homer Banks, Bettye Crutcher, Don Davis, Raymond Jackson. UK Owner: Rondor Music (London) Ltd.* 'Greased' Lightnin'' by John Travolta from *Grease (Original Soundtrack)* (Polydor, 1978): *Compl/Auth: Jim Jacobs, Warren Casey. UK Owner: Chappell Morris Ltd.* 'Something Came Over Me' from *Mission Of Dead Souls* by Throbbing Gristle (Mute, 1981): *Compl/Auth: Chris Carter, Cosey Newby, Peter Christopherson. UK Owner: Peermusic (UK) Ltd.* 'Red Light Special' from *CrazySexyCool* by TLC (La Face, 1994): *Compl/Auth: Kenneth Edmonds. UK Owner: Sony ATV Music Pub Ltd.* 'Jerk-Off' from *Opiate* by Tool (1992): *Compl/Auth: Tool.* 'Supermodel Sandwich w/Cheese' from *Terence Trent D'Arby's Vibrator* by Terence Trent D'Arby: (Columbia, 1995): *Compl/Auth: Terence Trent D'Arby. UK Owner: EMI Virgin Music Ltd.* 'Nann Nigga' from *www.thug.com* by Trick Daddy (featuring Trina) (Warlock, 1998): *Compl/Auth: Adam Duggins, Maurice Young. UK Owner: First and Gold Publishing.* 'Sex On The Beach' from *The Hit Collection* by T-Spoon (Remixed Records, 1997): *Compl/Auth: Serge Ramaekers, Domanic Sas, Remy De Groot,*

*Shalamon Baskin. UK Owner: EMI Music Publishing Ltd.* 'Me So Horny' from *As Nasty As They Wanna Be* by 2 Live Crew (Luke, 1989): *Comp/Auth: L Campbell, C Wongwon, D Hobbs, M Ross, R Williams. UK Owner: Universal MCA Music Ltd.* 'Thug Passion' from *All Eyez On Me* by 2 Pac (Death Row, 1996): *Comp/Auth: Tupac Shakur, Johnny Jackson, Larry Troutman, Roger Troutman, Shirley Murdock, Katari Cox, Malcolm Greenridge, Mutah Beale. UK Owner: Sony ATV Music Publishing Ltd.* 'Sorry' from *Unwritten Law* by Unwritten Law (Interscope, 1998): *Comp/Auth: Scott Russo, Robert Brewer, Steve Morris, Wade Youman, John Bell. UK Owner: Warner Chappell Music.* 'Sex Over The Phone' from *Sex Over The Phone* by Village People (Polygram, 1999): *Comp/Auth: Jaques Morali, Bruce Vilanch, Fred Zarr. UK Owner: EMI Music Publishing Ltd.* 'Big Long Sliding Thing' from *The Complete Dinah Washington On Mercury Vol. 3 (1952-54)* by Dinah Washington (Mercury, 1992): *Comp/Auth: Frank Thomas, Leroy Kirkland. UK Owner: IQ Music Ltd.* 'Animal (Fuck Like A Beast)' from *Animal (Fuck Like A Beast)* by W.A.S.P. (Restless, 1983): *Comp/Auth: Steve Duren. UK Owner: Zomba Music Publishing Ltd.* 'Organ Grinder Blues' from *The Chronological Ethel Waters: 1926-1929* by Ethel Waters (French Classics, 1974): *Comp/Auth: Clarence Williams. UK Owner: Redwood Music Ltd.* 'She Fucks Me' from *Paintin' The Town Brown - Ween Live (90-98)* by Ween (Mushroom, 1999): *Comp/Auth: Michael Melchiondo, Aaron Freeman. UK Owner: Warner Chappell Music.* 'It's Ecstasy When You Lay Down Next To Me' from *Barry White Sings For Someone You Love* by Barry White (A&M, 1977): *Comp/Auth: Nelson Pigford, Ekundayo Paris. UK Owner: Minder Music Ltd.* 'Hi Hi Hi' from *Wings Greatest* by Wings (EMI, 1978): *Comp/Auth: Paul McCartney, Linda McCartney. UK Owner: MPL Communications.* 'Totally Nude' from *All Hell's Breaking Loose Down At Little Kathy Wilson's Place* by Wolfsbane (Def American, 1990): *Comp/Auth: Bayley Cooke, Jason Edwards. UK Owner: American Def Tunes.* 'Rump Shaker' from *Hard Or Smooth* by Wreckx-N-Effect (MCA,1992): *Comp/Auth: Aqil Davidson, Teddy Riley, Markell Riley, Anton Hollins, David Wynn, Pharrell Williams, Lana Moorer, Freddie Bryd, David Porter. UK Owner: Rondor Music (London) Ltd.* 'Bang' from *Master* by Yeah Yeah Yeahs (Shifty, 2001): *Comp/Auth: Brian Chase, Nick Zinner.* 'Why Does It Hurt When I Pee?' from *Joe's Garage Act I* by Frank Zappa (Zappa Records, 1979): *Comp/Auth: Frank Zappa. UK Owner: Warner Chappell Music.* 'The Ballad Of Resurrection Joe And Rosa Whore' from *Hellbilly Deluxe* by Rob Zombie (Geffen, 1998): *Comp/Auth: Rob Zombie, Scott Hunphrey. UK Owner: Warner Chappell Music.*